Prostitution

IN THE
BASQUE COUNTRY
AND NEVADA

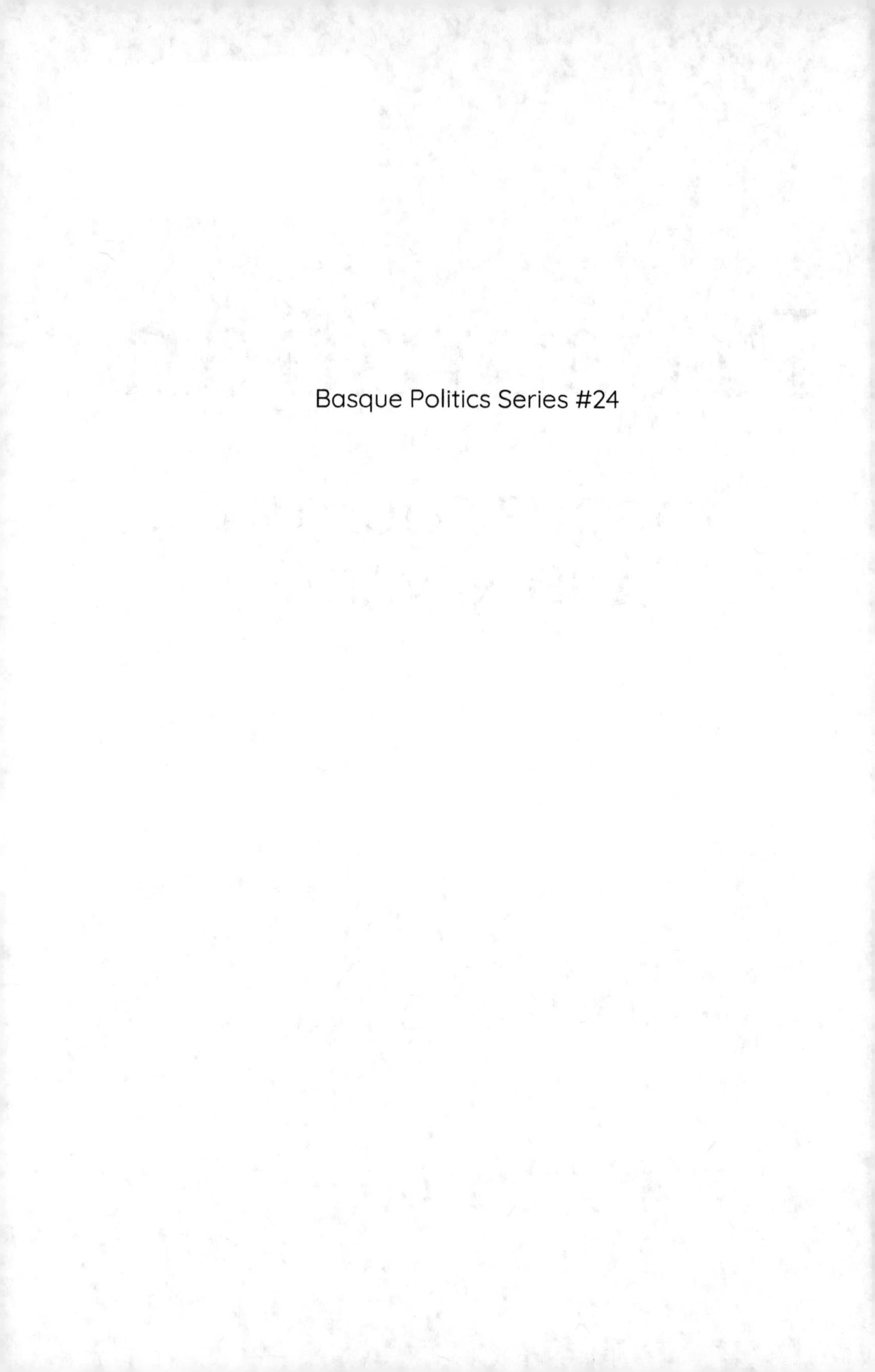

Basque Politics Series #24

Prostitution

IN THE
BASQUE COUNTRY
AND NEVADA

edited by

Xabier Irujo
Sarah Jane Blithe
Yolanda Rodríguez Villegas

CENTER FOR BASQUE STUDIES
UNIVERSITY OF NEVADA, RENO
2023

This book was published with generous financial support from the Basque Government.

Center for Basque Studies
University of Nevada, Reno
1664 North Virginia St,
Reno, Nevada 89557 usa
http://basque.unr.edu

Cover Design by Alissa Gates Booth

Library of Congress Cataloging-in-Publication Data

Names: Irujo Ametzaga, Xabier, editor. | Blithe, Sarah, editor. | Rodríguez, Yolanda, editor.
Title: Prostitution in the Basque country and Nevada / edited by Xabier Irujo, Sarah Blithe, Yolanda Rodriguez.
Description: 1 Edition. | Reno : Center for Basque Studies, [2023] | Series: Basque politics series; Book 24 | Includes bibliographical references and index. | Summary: "Across the globe, the "world's oldest profession" continues to ignite controversy and intrigue. Prostitution is a $186 billion dollar global industry that is characterized, practiced, and governed in highly disparate ways depending on the cultural and ideological context in which it is practiced. The scholars contributing to this volume span multiple countries and take up vastly different perspectives about sex work. The cultural framings of prostitution in the Basque country are quite different from how prostitution is framed in Nevada- the only state in the United States where prostitution is not illegal in a few areas. In some ways, prostitution is similar in both contexts: there are advocates for sex work as work in both locations, and there are anti-prostitution advocates in both contexts as well. Further, sex workers around the world face a higher risk of violence, stigma, and moral judgments about their character that can impede their everyday life experiences regardless of geographical location"-- Provided by publisher.
Identifiers: LCCN 2023010012 (print) | LCCN 2023010013 (ebook) | ISBN 9781949805734 (paperback) | ISBN 9781949805758 (epub)
Subjects: LCSH: Prostitution--Cross-cultural studies. | Prostitution--Law and legislation--Cross-cultural studies. | Prostitutes--Social conditions--Cross-cultural studies. | Women--Violence against.
Classification: LCC HQ118 .P7676 2023 (print) | LCC HQ118 (ebook) | DDC 306.74--dc23/ eng/20230310
LC record available at https://lccn.loc.gov/2023010012
LC ebook record available at https://lccn.loc.gov/2023010013

Printed in the United States of America

Contents

Prologue *by Xabier Irujo, Sarah Jane Blithe, and Yolanda Rodríguez Villegas* ....*vii*

Chapter 1: (De)Criminalization of Sex Work: Sex Workers' Experiences in Nepal and Nevada *by Rebecca J. Meisenbach, Sydney Graham, Yerina S. Ranjit, and Omita Joshi* *1*

Chapter 2: Fractured Organizational Support for Sex Workers *by Sarah Jane Blithe and Tennley A. Vik* *22*

Chapter 3: Sex Work is Real Work: Benefits and Obstacles to Personal Autonomy in the Sex Industry *by Amelia Walker* *40*

Chapter 4: Prostitution in the Basque Country (Euskal Herria) *by Xabier Irujo* *67*

Chapter 5: Social Imaginaries of Prostitution: Transferences in the Circle of Sexual Victimization *by Silvia Pérez Freire* *91*

Chapter 6: The New Abolitionism Model *by Yolanda Rodríguez Villegas* *108*

Biographies *129*

Index *132*

Prologue

Xabier Irujo
Sarah Jane Blithe
Yolanda Rodríguez Villegas

Across the globe, the "world's oldest profession" continues to ignite controversy and intrigue. Prostitution is a $186 billion global industry that is characterized, practiced, and governed in highly disparate ways depending on the cultural and ideological context in which it is conducted.[1] Researching prostitution and advocating for sex workers are difficult tasks. Sex workers are often hidden from mainstream society, engaging in either illegal or legal but highly stigmatized work. To complicate scholarship, prostitution is wrapped up in a web of contradictory perspectives, conflated terms, misinformation, and deeply engrained moral judgments about intimacy, exploitation, empowerment, and sin.[2]

Taking an international perspective to sex work reveals the very complicated nature of the industry. Sex workers are subject to a vast array of laws and governance that dictate how prostitution occurs. People engage in prostitution for myriad complicated reasons. Culture certainly plays an important role in how people get into prostitution, but also families, economic status, and intersections of social identity, such as race, sexuality, and gender identity are important factors in how and why people become sex workers. These factors are also important for understanding the type of experiences individual sex workers might have. Sex workers of color and trans sex workers experience higher rates of violence and death, while white, legal brothel workers report a much safer, more lucrative experience. Prostitutes working on streets experience significantly higher rates of violence and stigma than do prostitutes who work indoors.[3]

The term "sex work" is an umbrella term for a variety of occupations, including exotic dancing, prostitution, pornography, telephone sex, sex paraphernalia sales, escorting, and sugaring (a transactional dating practice typically characterized by an older, wealthier person and a younger person in need of financial assistance). Each of these occupations offers different benefits, drawbacks, and contexts. While "sex work" as a term is less precise, it is also the term with which most prostitutes in the United States identify. It is used politically to signal the support of sex work as a viable occupation and as a way to avoid the stigma attached to the word "prostitute." At the same time, some advocates insist on using the term "prostitute" or "prostituted woman" to signal their belief that consent to the sale of sex is impossible. The term "prostitute" itself is less offensive in other parts of the world than it is in the US. Throughout this book, both terms are used. In some cases, the political standpoint of the authors is clearly indicated by their choice of term. In other cases, "prostitution" is used to describe a particular type of sex work. Here, we use both terms for precision and in describing multiple uses of these contested terms.

Sex workers are considered dirty workers[4]—people who engage in "disgusting" or degrading work and who are stigmatized for their occupation. Organization scholars Blake Ashforth and Glen Kreiner argued that dirty workers are tainted by the physically, socially, emotionally, and morally objectionable tasks they complete at work.[5] Physical taint describes work that requires close proximity to a noxious substance such as garbage or waste. Social taint describes contact with people who are considered disgusting or dangerous. Emotional taint occurs when workers must engage in high levels of emotional display or in highly emotional contexts.[6] Moral taint describes activity that is deemed sinful.[7] The stigma experienced by sex workers is among the most oppressive in all occupations. Sex workers also experience symbolic stigma[8] because they are considered a health threat to society, and whore stigma[9] because they sell sexual experiences. Sex workers experience layers of stigma that affect their ability to exist in society safely and without judgment.

Advocates take a number of perspectives to understand sex work. These ideological positions determine not only how one views prostitution, but they also drive legislation about sex work. For decades, advocates from multiple groups have been entrenched in debates about the nature of prostitution, consent, choice, occupation, and exploitation.

Radical libertarian or "sex positive" advocates view sex as a powerful and liberating experience for women. They applaud sex workers for engaging in a freely chosen career that can fulfill their sexual needs and infuse power in women taking charge of a sexual situation.[10] These advocates believe that women can consent to sex work as a viable economic choice to earn good wages. Proponents of decriminalization argue that sex work will occur in any context, and that sex workers experience a greater proportion of stigma and violence because of laws that criminalize prostitution. They argue that police often perpetuate violence by arresting people involved in sex work, and suggest that funds currently allocated for policing could be better used for education and social services.[11] Further, proponents of decriminalization believe that criminalization drives prostitution underground, which in turn puts sex workers in more dangerous situations. Also included in the collective of advocates who are against the criminalization of prostitution are those in favor of legalization. People who support the legalization of prostitution draw many of the same arguments as those who support decriminalization. However, they also support laws, taxation, and other forms of regulation on the sex industry.

Anti-prostitution groups, on the other hand, often assume that all prostitution is exploitative. Activists following this ideology are either abolitionists (believing that all forms of prostitution should be abolished) or prohibitionist (believing that prostitution should be prohibited). The difference between the two has to do with law; prohibitionists would make the exchange of money for sexual services explicitly illegal or prohibited. Abolitionists seek to completely abolish the institution of prostitution in all forms. People taking up anti-prostitution positions are sometimes unlikely collaborators—radical feminists and religious groups. Among other concerns, radical-cultural feminists believe that sex is always possession and violence over women. Their main objection to sex work is the perceived dominance of women. Whereas, religious advocates take a moral objection to sex outside of sanctioned marriages, or sex with multiple partners, among other moral objections. Advocates taking these perspectives often equate all paid sex work as exploitative, and believe that consent is impossible in an exploitative context. In this light, all prostitution is trafficking.

The issue of trafficking is a thorny problem for both groups. Anti-prostitution advocates often claim that because it can never be freely chosen, all prostitution is trafficking. These groups have been accused of inflating trafficking numbers and creating dramatized stories about young white women kidnapped and sold into prostitution—a scenario that remains quite rare. Anti-prostitution advocates are also accused of overlooking chattel slavery, particularly in highly visible "sexual slavery" campaigns. On the other hand, decriminalization advocates are accused of overlooking trafficking victims and minimizing trafficking in general. In truth, the number of people engaging in prostitution by their own free will and the number of people trafficked for forced sex work are almost impossible to track. Statistics vary widely and are difficult to obtain. Individual countries report a range of trafficking cases—from fewer than one hundred people annually to three hundred thousand annually. Much of this disparity in statistics lies in the ideological perspective of prostitution.

The scholars contributing to this volume span multiple countries and take up vastly different perspectives about sex work. The cultural framings of prostitution in the Basque Country are quite different from how prostitution is framed in Nevada—the only state in the United States where prostitution is not illegal in a few areas. In some ways, prostitution is similar in both contexts: there are advocates for sex work as *work* in both locations, and there are anti-prostitution advocates in both contexts as well. Further, sex workers around the world face a higher risk of violence, stigma, and moral judgments about their character that can impede their everyday life experiences regardless of geographical location.

Prostitution in Nevada includes illegal prostitution, occurring often on streets and in hotels. It also includes legal prostitution in permitted brothels. There are only about twenty brothels in the state. Most of these locations are small operations—a few sex workers in a trailer or small building. A few brothels are large, resort-like places that can accommodate more than fifty sex workers. Brothel sex workers are subject to different rules and regulations, depending on the city and county in which the brothel is located. Legal prostitutes in Nevada are independent contractors. As such, they are supposed to be able to decide the hours and days they work. However, some women experience lockdown—rules that prohibit sex workers to leave the brothel grounds without a chaperone during their contract period. Others have claimed that they are required to work particular shifts.[12]

The analysis of prostitution in the Basque Country must be placed within the European sociocultural and legal paradigm, where it is increasingly understood that prostitution is synonymous with human trafficking and exploitation. In the Basque case, not all prostitution is trafficking, but the vast majority is. The social cause that underlies is fundamentally the feminization of poverty. In the European context, abolition and prohibition are not synonyms. Abolitionists consider that the prostitution system is a foundational institution of patriarchy. From this perspective, if those who are prostituted are women (95 percent of the cases) and those who prostitute are men (in 99 percent of the cases), prostitution is one more example of the structural inequality between women and men and, therefore, it must disappear. A number of European countries have passed legislation to abolish sexual exploitation, and in the Basque Country legal measures have been taken to abolish prostitution. The concept "sex worker" is a controversial term in Europe linked to a specific ideological trend—regulationism. In general terms, the term used to make reference to prostitutes is "prostituted women."

The chapters in this book analyze prostitution in a wide range of contexts. The first half of the book focuses primarily on sex work in the United States. In the first chapter, Rebecca J. Meisenbach, Sydney Graham, Yerina S. Ranjit, and Omita Joshi argue for increased attention to how organizational and governmental structures relate to sex work stigma. By comparing communication and disclosure practices of sex workers in legal brothels in Nevada with the experiences of illegal street-based sex workers in Nepal, they explore intersections of criminalization, pride, shame, and occupational stigma. The analysis highlights how legalization and criminalization structure sex workers' agency and choices, including where and how they obtain personal and health support, and why and how they conceal or proclaim their sex work identities.

In chapter 2, Tennley A. Vik and Sarah Jane Blithe analyze organizations that exist to support sex workers around the world. They analyze sex worker support organizations with anti-prostitution missions, sex workers' rights organizations, and sex worker health organizations and find different goals and methods for providing support. The authors argue that ideological differences among the organizations fracture the type of support offered to sex workers.

Amelia Walker explores the interrelationships between prominent ideologies, power relationships, and shared phenomena in her critical thematic analysis of a sex work panel on Reddit. She found that exploitation, sex work versus trafficking, criminalization, job autonomy, pleasure, stigma, sex work is work, morality, income (in)stability, censorship, and marginalization were important themes that sex workers presented. Ultimately, she relates the Reddit themes with larger ideologies, and she discusses the policy implications for sex workers and trafficking survivors.

The second half of the book explores prostitution in the Basque Country and other European contexts. First, Xabier Irujo argues that prostitution has a global reach, and that each place has its own peculiarities, not only relating to the origin of the prostituted women, but also in terms of the characteristics of the prostitutes, the networks of pimping, the juridical and legal context, and its social implantation. He argues that all of these factors depend in sum of the tolerance, normalization, trivialization, or rejection that society presents when confronting this expression of patriarchal violence. He describes the legal aspects of prostitution in both the Southern and Northern Basque Country and includes data from the Southern part of the country, such as the number of women who are being prostituted, their place of origin, the networks that bring them to the Basque Country, the methods implanted for their recruitment, the characteristics of the consumers and, finally, what is being done, by action or omission, from the institutions to deter or put an end to the sexual exploitation of women.

Silvia Pérez Freire analyzes how the patriarchal contexts in which the different types of sex trade develop in current societies (prostitution, sexual exploitation, sex trafficking), and the divergent judicial-political responses (legalize, tolerate, punish) unequivocally contribute to a sociocultural construct of vague social imaginary that function to neutralize any criticism regarding these phenomena. She argues that what the so-called first-order observers (social agents directly linked to this social reality: public institutions, legal system and the police, specialized nongovernmental organizations, professional experts, client/pimps, and victims) say, do, and narrate constitute diverse social systems, which serve to represent the social imaginary that enables feedback in the circle of sexual victimization, where the victim is vilified and the criminal becomes the victim of sex trafficking. This entrenches patriarchal woman/perverse whore myths, and expunges/transfers the social and individual responsibility of the dubiously perceived harm and psychological injury resulting from prostitution.

Finally, Yolanda Rodríguez Villegas deconstructs the New Abolitionist Model. In 1999, the Law of Peace for Women was passed in Sweden, a law that included prostitution as a form of gender violence. For the first time, the law did not criminalize prostituted women, but rather persecuted procurers and users, that is, those who organized or made use of prostitution. Twenty-one years later, and after several countries of the European Union approved abolitionist laws, a proposal for an Organic Law for the Abolition of the Prostitution System was passed in the Spanish state that revolves around three fundamental axes—the guarantee of the fundamental rights of prostituted women; prevention, awareness, education, and training of all the actors involved in the prostitution system; and the disincentive for the demand and the prosecution of pimping.

Taken together, the chapters in this book present the complicated and interesting picture of prostitution in multiple locations across the globe. The authors have distinctly different social and occupational identities, different perspectives about prostitution, and varied ideas about how to best support sex workers. Because of the stigmatizing nature of prostitution, producing scholarship that provides a nuanced perspective can be difficult and threatening to identities. As such, we thank the authors for putting forward their expertise and experiences to make this volume complete.

REFERENCES

Ashforth, Blake E., and Glen E. Kreiner. " 'How can you do it?': Dirty work and the challenge of constructing a positive identity." *Academy of Management Review* 24, no. 3 (1999): 413–434.

Blithe, Sarah Jane, Anna Wiederhold Wolfe, and Breanna Mohr. *Sex and Stigma: Stories of Everyday Life in Nevada's Legal Brothels.* NYU Press, 2019.

Brents, Barbara G., and Kathryn Hausbeck. "Violence and legalized brothel prostitution in Nevada: Examining safety, risk, and prostitution policy." *Journal of Interpersonal Violence* 20, no. 3 (2005): 270-295.

Global Health Justice Partnership. "Protecting the health and rights of sex workers in the US and globally," Yale Law School, accessed October 11, 2021 https://law.yale.edu/ghjp/projects/gender-sexuality-and-rights/protecting-health-and-rights-sex-workers-us-and-globally.

Havocscope. "Prostitution: Prices and statistics of the global sex trade." (2013).

Herek, G.M., K.F. Widaman, and J.P. Capitanio. 2005. "When sex equals AIDS: Symbolic stigma and heterosexual adults' inaccurate beliefs about sexual transmission of AIDS." *Social Problems* 52 (1): 15–37.

Hughes, Everett Cherrington. "Work and the self." (1951).

McMurray, Robert, and Jenna Ward. "'Why would you want to do that?': Defining emotional dirty work." *Human Relations* 67, no. 9 (2014): 1123–1143.

Pheterson, Gail. 1993. "The whore stigma: female dishonor and male unworthiness." *Social Text* 37: 39–64.

NOTES

1　Havocscope. "Prostitution: Prices and Statistics of the Global Sex Trade." (2013).

2　Blithe, Sarah Jane, Anna Wiederhold Wolfe, and Breanna Mohr. *Sex and Stigma: Stories of Everyday Life in Nevada's Legal Brothels.* NYU Press, 2019.

3　Brents, Barbara G., and Kathryn Hausbeck. "Violence and legalized brothel prostitution in Nevada: Examining safety, risk, and prostitution policy." *Journal of Interpersonal Violence* 20, no. 3 (2005): 270-295.

4　Hughes, Everett Cherrington. "Work and the self." (1951).

5　Ashforth, Blake E., and Glen E. Kreiner. " 'How can you do it?': Dirty work and the challenge of constructing a positive identity." *Academy of Management Review* 24, no. 3 (1999): 413–434.

6　McMurray, Robert, and Jenna Ward. "'Why would you want to do that?': Defining emotional dirty work." *Human Relations* 67, no. 9 (2014): 1123–1143.

7　Ashforth, Blake E., and Glen E. Kreiner. " 'How can you do it?': Dirty work and the challenge of constructing a positive identity." *Academy of Management Review* 24, no. 3 (1999): 413–434.

8   Herek, G.M., K.F. Widaman, and J.P. Capitanio. 2005. "When sex equals AIDS: Symbolic stigma and heterosexual adults' inaccurate beliefs about sexual transmission of AIDS." *Social Problems* 52 (1): 15–37.

9   Pheterson, Gail. 1993. "The whore stigma: Female dishonor and male unworthiness." *Social Text* 37: 39–64.

10   Blithe et al., *Sex and Stigma*.

11   Global Health Justice Partnership, https://law.yale.edu/ghjp/projects/gender-sexuality-and-rights/protecting-health-and-rights-sex-workers-us-and-globally.

12   Blithe et al., *Sex and Stigma*.

Chapter 1

(De)Criminalization of Sex Work

Sex Workers' Experiences in Nepal and Nevada

Rebecca J. Meisenbach
Sydney Graham
Yerina S. Ranjit
Omita Joshi

Sex work and stigma have long been uncomfortably linked around the world. Sex work is generally understood as the exchange of money for consensual sexual activity, a category that tends to include stripping, exotic dancing, and prostitution. Countries and governments assign sex work various legal statuses that intersect with public and cultural attitudes. In most places, the dominant public attitude toward sex work is negative, aligning with research on stigma and stigmatized occupations, in which stigma is understood as a communication process that discredits individuals associated with a negatively perceived characteristic. Prior research suggests that criminalization and stigmas decrease sex workers' access to and use of health services and protective practices (Bekker et al. 2015). We extend this research by focusing on and comparing how female identified sex workers in a legalized sex work environment and those in an ambiguously criminalized environment experience stigma and health support.

Issues of sex work legality meaningfully connect with research on dirty work, which addresses occupations and roles that are likely to be perceived as disgusting or degrading (Ashforth and Kreiner 1999). Based on the work of sociologist Everett Hughes (e.g., 1958), dirty work research attends to physical, social, and moral sources of taint associated with members of certain occupations and to how individuals manage them (e.g., Ashforth and Kreiner 1999). Physical taint refers to how jobs may be dangerous and/or literally engage with dirt, body fluids, and other unpleasant physical elements. Social taint references work that involves the worker being subservient to another, and moral taint addresses how some jobs require the worker to violate community standards of what is seen as right and good. Sex work is affected by all three sources of taint in some ways and, thus, has been a frequent site of dirty work research (e.g., Benoit et al. 2021; Grandy and Mavin 2014). Interestingly, Ashforth and Kreiner (2014) argued that in contrast to the perceived necessity of physical and social dirty work in society, that "moral dirty work tends to be seen as more evil than necessary. Moral dirty work typically constitutes a graver identity threat to occupational members" (100). Sex work is less often framed as necessary, and thus, the moral taint may well be the strongest source of stigma for sex workers. This moral taint has implications for how sex work is legislated and for how sex workers manage their occupational identities and health care choices. In what follows we consider these conditions and experiences in Nepal and Nevada.

THE CONFUSING CRIMINALIZATION OF PROSTITUTION IN NEPAL

Nepal is a country of twenty-seven million people who represent at least 125 ethnic groups. About 25 percent of the nation's population lives below the poverty line. Its capital city of Kathmandu is home to two and a half million people, and 16,000-18,000 of those residents are believed to be involved in sex work (Tanaka, 2020). Indeed, for many women in lower castes in Nepal, prostitution (the exchange of sexual acts for money) is viewed as one of the only viable paths for making enough money to support their families, even as overall in Nepal, sex work "is a social taboo" and is viewed as "an act against the morality of the people" (Raut 2015, 187).

In comparison to the clear criminality of sex work in many countries, the legality/criminality of sex work in Nepal is nebulous. As Raut (2015) noted, "Nepal is the country which has neither criminalized nor legalized nor decriminalized the sex work" (200), that is, Nepal does not have laws that explicitly and specifically criminalize sex workers. Yet, several laws create a culture in which communities and the sex workers themselves may perceive sex work as criminalized. For example, as far back as 1970, sex workers have been arrested via the

Public Offense and Penalties Act's prohibition of obscene acts and words in public places (Tanaka 2020).

As elsewhere, sex work in Nepal is sometimes viewed as illegal through its conflation with human trafficking. For example, a subsection of Nepal's Human Trafficking and Transportation Act of 2007 designated engagement in prostitution as unlawful (section 15.d). This line in the law has been interpreted in multiple ways, with some suggesting it criminalizes the purchase of sex and not the sex worker (known as the Swedish model as a nod to Sweden's early use of this practice). This interpretation aligns with the agenda of scholars and activists who favor abolishing prostitution. However, in practice, the law in Nepal can also be interpreted to mean that the sex worker is subject to the penalties as well as someone who "engages" in prostitution. In a third interpretation, sex worker rights advocates in Nepal argue that the law is about those who have been sex trafficked and does not apply to those engaged in voluntary sex work. More recent legislation has only further increased perceptions of sex work as unlawful. For example, Nepal's Criminal Act (2017) makes it illegal to advertise for sex work or to provide house, land, or vehicles "for the purpose of whoredom and prostitution" (120 and 120.1.1.).

Several groups in Nepal today emphasize and advocate for decriminalization without legalization of sex work. One of the key arguments from these groups against legalization is that such moves are likely to still exclude the most vulnerable sex workers, who include the housewives, migrants, and transgender women we interviewed in Nepal. As part of considering the possibilities of legalized prostitution for sex workers, we turn to Nevada's brothel system.

LEGALIZED PROSTITUTION IN NEVADA'S BROTHELS

Unlike Nepal, the United States is clear about its criminalization of sex work in most of the country. Sex workers, pimps, and all other members of the industry can be charged as criminals. The state of Nevada, however, is an exception to this norm. In ten of the seventeen Nevada counties, sex work is legal in licensed brothel houses (solicitation of sex work outside of a licensed brothel house is still prohibited) (NRS 201.354). Since the 1850s, places of prostitution have operated in Nevada, and today about twenty brothels operate throughout the state. Nevada state law prohibits brothels in counties that exceed 700,000 residents (Clark County, which includes the city of Las Vegas, is the only county with a population of more than 700,000); therefore, the brothels exist in more rural Nevada communities (NRS 244.345; Wolfe and Blithe 2015). These communities benefit greatly from the tax benefits associated with the brothels (Brents, Jackson, and Hausbeck 2009).

Although sex workers are employed by brothel houses, these individuals must register as independent contractors and obtain a work card (also known as a "sheriff's card") from the local police or sheriff's office (Brents, Jackson, and Hausback 2009; NRS 244.345; Wolfe and Blithe 2015). In addition, sex workers are legally required to pass weekly and monthly health testing for sexually transmitted infections. Positive results make them ineligible to work. For example, they are prohibited from working if they have tested positive for HIV (Brents, Jackson, and Hausbeck 2009; NRS 201.358).

In addition to adhering to state, county, and city laws, sex workers must follow rules within their specific brothels. These rules might include lockdown policies or restrictions on their travel. For example, lockdown policies may require that legal sex workers stay at the brothel from 5 p.m. to 8 a.m. or from 8 a.m. to 7 p.m. (Blithe and Wolfe 2017). Some brothels require that sex workers be accompanied by "runners" when leaving brothel grounds during a contract period. Many brothels provide extensive amenities and services (including onsite health care) that ensure sex workers do not have to leave brothel grounds often, if at all, during their contract period. As contract workers, however, they typically must purchase their own regular health care insurance.

Despite this legalized environment, much of the social and moral taint surrounding sex work in the US and Nevada is still rooted in assumptions that all sex workers are victims; sex work and sex trafficking are the same; and sex work is immoral (Blithe and Wolfe 2017; McCarthy et al. 2012). Further, the morally conservative viewpoint assumes society needs protection from sex workers because of disease, drug use, and other criminal activities (Blithe and Wolfe 2017; Miller and Haltiwanger 2004). As in Nepal, those in the sex work industry in the US debate which type of regulation, if any, is preferred (e.g., Lutnick and Cohan 2009). For example, some people do not want the strict supervision of the legalized industry while others prefer the safety protocols and amenities provided in legal brothels.

METHODS

This chapter incorporates data from two separate research projects to address the identities, experiences, and stigmatization of two groups of female-identified sex workers. The focus groups and interviews used helped researchers understand what experiences and ideas are particularly meaningful to participants.

The focus groups in Nepal were conducted in 2020-2021 as part of a larger project focused on the health care and safety needs of FSWs (female-identified sex workers) in Nepal. The overall project seeks to better understand the role of stigma in sex work and health care, with a goal of designing a mobile phone-based intervention to improve their experiences, including through preventing and treating HIV and other sexually transmitted infections.

The US interview data was collected in 2018 as part of the second author's master's thesis research on identity tensions of stigmatized workers. The original study explored how legal sex workers interpret discourses of occupational shaming and stigma and how those interpretations shape occupational identification, self-identity, and self-image.

PARTICIPANTS

The first dataset consists of four focus groups with FSWs from Kathmandu, Nepal. In total, thirty-two FSWs participated, with an average age of twenty-nine and an average of five years of experience in sex work. One focus group consisted solely of transgender FSWs, while the other three focus groups comprised cisgender FSWs.

The US data consist of in-depth interviews conducted by the second author with nine legal female sex workers and two female brothel madams at four brothels outside of Reno, Nevada, and one brothel in Elko County, Nevada. Participants had from eleven months to eighteen years of experience in the industry, with an average of six years. The brothel madams had been in the industry for twenty-five to thirty years.

NEPAL DATA PROCEDURES

The recruitment process for the focus groups in Nepal involved several stages. First, the research team established contacts at a local nongovernmental health and social programming organization called Communication Action Center (CAC)-Nepal, based in Kathmandu. This organization has been providing services for economically disadvantaged women in the Kathmandu Valley for the past twenty-eight years. A CAC-Nepal staff member (the fourth author of this chapter) approached FSWs in various urban slum locations in Kathmandu, where CAC-Nepal had previously provided health and other social services to women.

The focus group discussions were conducted in locations easily accessible to FSWs, such as a storage room for a local shop in the slum area and an office space of a nonprofit organization for the LGBTQ community. Participants were compensated $4.42 USD or Nepali Rupees (NRs. 500) for their time.

The focus groups each had five to ten participants and lasted an average of sixty-seven minutes. Focus groups were audio-recorded and transcribed verbatim in Nepali by a native language speaker, translated into English, then checked by the third author. The first author, who is a native English speaker and does not speak Nepali, read the transcripts and made notes about any confusing wording. The third author then revised the transcripts if additional translational work was appropriate.

NEVADA DATA

The second author recruited participants through cold-calling and local contacts. Interviews were conducted in brothel common spaces or private rooms. Interviews lasted an average of fifty-two minutes. After leaving the field, the interview files were transcribed verbatim by the second author.

In the sections that follow, all participants' identities are anonymized. Nevada interview participants are identified via a pseudonym. Nepalese focus group participants are identified by their focus group number (i.e., Participant#/FocusGroup#).

ANALYSIS TECHNIQUES

The first author inductively analyzed all the transcripts of the interviews and focus groups, focusing on discussions of legality, stigma, and disclosure. The first and second authors explored the range of responses in each area, seeking similarities and differences within and across the two data sets. Initial coding suggested concerns about disclosure decisions surrounding their sex worker identity, health care, and the legalization/(de)criminalization of sex work. The first and second authors then reread the data and highlighted quotes relevant to these three themes. During this step, we constructed subcategories related to safety, blackmail, interactions with police, and sex work advocacy. We then selected quotes illustrating the range of responses related to each theme. The next section shares our analysis of these themes.

DISCLOSURE OF SEX WORK IDENTITY

For the Nepali FSWs, disclosure decisions were closely tied to their needs for safety and privacy. The legal and moral judgments against sex work in Nepal meant that most participants tried to maintain secrecy, even from their families, about their participation in sex work. Many described being purposefully vague about their work or pretending to be going to another place for work. A few also worked in other more respected jobs and thus, they simply pretended or implied that that was their only job. They engaged in these avoiding behaviors because they expected their families, homes, and communities would ostracize them if they were known as a FSW. For example, P4 and P8 discussed what would happen if anyone where they lived knew:

> **P4:** Fight may arouse due to that . . .
> **P8:** They kick us out of the house, they kick us out of the village.
> **P4:** The house owner would kick us out of the room if they would know about us. (FG1)

The transgender FSWs (many of whom were married to women) reported similar secrecy, though some of their secrecy was about HIV status as much as their sex worker identities:

> We only tell things like this or are open about it in the office (LGBTQI office) only. But our family, neighbors don't know that I have been affected by this [HIV]. If anyone knows about this, then it would be a problem, right? People will say, "Your son has been transmitted with this disease; how did it transmit?" This will create a problem to their father and mother, too. (P2/FG3)

In such scenarios, being known to be HIV positive was a path to revealing their association with other stigmatized characteristics (i.e., homosexuality and sex work) since many assume that these identities and practices cause HIV positive status.

As a result of the FSWs' desire to hide their sex work identity, blackmail threats from clients are a common and real problem. Many participants viewed blackmail as an inevitable part of their lives: "If we tell the reality [that we are FSWs], then it is obvious that the person will blackmail us" (P7/FG4). The threat of eviction resulting from this identity disclosure to family members and landlords limits the choices the FSWs perceive that they have about when and with whom they engage in sex work, as seen in this exchange in FG4:

> **P1:** If we say we don't want to work one day, . . . it is not possible because they call us and threaten us saying, "Now I will tell your family, I will do this, I will out you in media. If you won't come, I will do this."

> **P7:** They blackmail us. Yes, that is why knowing that [about our sex work], they start blackmailing, "I will talk about you in your house [tell your family]." We get afraid, and we can't say anything out of fear. He might also start blackmailing us to pay him money.
> **P5:** We get stuck in swamp.
> **P4:** Also, due to fear that they will tell to our family, we are compelled to go to them. We have to go . . .
> **P3:** We have to go wherever we are told to come.

Several participants discussed how videos and pictures of their sex work interactions were part of the blackmail, but some noted that such blackmail can go both ways, particularly among transgender sex workers and their clients:

> **P2:** I was talking about blackmailing, related to mobile phones. When we go to meet someone without knowing them or an anonymous person and when it's the first time you are going to have a sexual relation with them the clients make sex videos. So, they often use such videos to blackmail us; such cases happen.
> **P4:** People from our community [sex workers] sometimes take photos and call clients in the room and take sex videos. After which they use to bargain for more money by saying, "Give me more money, otherwise I will leak your photos and videos." We've heard such rumors as well in our community of a case or two. (FG3)

As seen in this exchange, in the case of transgender sex work, the related stigma of homosexuality affects both the client and the sex worker, making each more vulnerable to the other in terms of disclosure. In contrast, the male clients who are having sex with female sex workers appear to be unconcerned about how their own reputation might be affected by disclosing *how* they know that a woman is a sex worker.

Alongside this blackmail, the FSWs also talked about receiving death threats from clients who have access to their mobile numbers:

> **P4:** Sometimes someone wins the heart and later the same person searches for us through the SIM card and says, "Where are you? I will kill you," they say so—

Speaker unclear: "I'm going to kill you; you keep roaming with someone else, I will cut your legs." They [clients] say so, but if we don't use the same SIM whom will they call and threaten of cutting legs? (Everyone laughs)

This macabre humor makes sense as they seek to cope with the violence and precarious sense of safety they live with daily.

The legal sex workers in Nevada are also concerned about their privacy and safety, but the experiences and expressions of those concerns in their sex identity disclosures are distinct. The LFSWs believed in maintaining some level of privacy, including hiding their legal names, phone numbers, and personal email addresses. Beyond this baseline, their disclosure stances and strategies varied. Andie, one of the most successful sex workers in the industry, has disclosed her sex worker identity to the majority of people in her life:

> I do believe in having that separation, but my name is out there, my face is out there, my email is out there. I ... do ... everything [marketing]. My whole family knows, my friends know, my doctor knows, my dentist knows, my beautician knows, my hair stylist knows, my nail tech knows, my dog sitter knows, my house keepers know. Everybody, literally, anybody who is in my life ... the people who I see all the time. My waitress at Denny's knows.

Others discussed how their less open disclosure decisions were based on safety and privacy. For example, Cara shared:

> It's not like I'm going to be telling this whole world because it's more of a safety and privacy issue. I provide very intimate services, and some men fall for the fantasy, so they'll get obsessive or they just want to know more so I have to think ... I need my privacy in some areas of my life because it's when I don't have privacy, it's a safety issue.

The majority of these women used stage names and were active on social media under those names while on contract, but were less open when off contract. For example, Natalie said:

> I think that the wrong person finding out ... they can, it's always that sort of looming threat of sexual harassment or

something like that, too. Some random person I don't know can come up to me who found out through a friend of a friend of a friend, and just be creepy. It just comes with the territory. People just try to abuse the knowledge that they gain and, yeah, that's my biggest fear.

For those who chose to conceal their sex worker identity from family and friends, many attributed that secrecy to religious affiliation and disapproval. Natalie continued:

I have a very conservative family. So this would be something that would not be okay. . . . It's never fun to lie to them about what I do, but it's honestly for the best. . . . It's one of those situations where it's better left unsaid. It'd be like the final nail on the coffin sort of thing if I were to say, "Hey, this is what I'm doing." . . . So it's just better left unsaid.

Nicki, who has worked as a porn star and sex worker, also concealed her sex worker identity from her parents, but shared how her daughter found out:

My parents don't know what I do. They're very conservative. It's better that they don't know. I don't want [my mom] to go all teary eyed and everything. My daughter knows. Let me tell you how she found out. She went out with her boyfriend and everything. He pops on a DVD, and guess who was on the DVD? Mommy. She calls me. She goes, "Mom, really?" She took off. There was that little friction there for a while, but now she understands. When he put on that DVD, oh, my God, I had an earful! "How can you do this?" Blah, blah, blah. So yeah, she's from . . . a strict, like, Catholic upbringing, too, but now she kind of makes up for it, too. Now she's got tattoos and everything.

Many sex workers waited to share their work with friends and family until they were already working. For example, Angela shared:

I waited two weeks from the time I got here before I told my friends and family what I was up to. And that was just because I basically wanted it to be, one, too late for them to argue with

> me, and two, be able to say, "Yeah, it's safe and perfectly fine.
> I'm not in any danger. There are a million things I could be
> doing that you wouldn't think twice about that would be way
> more dangerous than this, so everything is fine." I wanted to
> be able to kind of just verify what I . . . my expectation that I
> thought it would be, well, well run and be safe, everything will
> be taken care of.

Her family responded positively to her disclosure and offered to help out with any difficulties the travel created. Their only sign of disappointment was that they wished she were working closer to home.

INTERACTIONS WITH LAW ENFORCEMENT AND THE LAW

The ambiguous nature of the laws regarding prostitution in Nepal, discussed earlier in this chapter, make it unsurprising that these FSWs' relationships with law enforcement are complicated and conflicting. They are often detained, but no one told stories of themselves or their friends being jailed long term. Instead they share stories of raids and "arrests" as one participant shared:

> What happened is . . . I was given the number of a room finder.
> . . . The "Akhtiyar" [corruption police] came to me. . . . They
> arrested me and kept me in their vehicle. . . . Once it was eve-
> ning . . . at seven o'clock, I went to [the prison]. I did my signa-
> ture there, and then I was allowed to go (P3/FG2).

Later when this group discussed how often they are robbed, several noted how the police often side with those who steal from and threaten FSWs ("Now police are also involved with those rascals" P6/FG2). The transgender FSWs discussed similar experiences: "There are many nighttime sex workers who get chased by the police on streets and are not allowed to be on the streets" (P4/FG3). Yet, they might also go to those police for help, as when one participant had two men on the street steal their mobile phone. The police helped them confront the thieves and retrieve the phone.

The conflicting nature of these FSWs' interactions with law enforcement are encapsulated in one FSW's (P9/FG4) story. She went to the police to try to stop her neighbors from harassing her with their accusations that she was a sex worker. The police sided with her community members in several ways: "When I filed the case . . . you know what the police said? . . . He said, 'When you live in a society, you cannot do degrading work.'" But eventually the police intervened, and the police said, 'From now onward, they will not abuse you under any circumstances' . . . they swear on police and also touched my feet . . . that was the condition . . . and after that once again [it happened]." Her experience shows the challenges of enforcing equal treatment for FSWs in Nepal: even after the community members are made to apologize to her and submissively touch her feet in front of the police, the harassing behavior continued.

In contrast, the interviews with Nevada's legal sex workers barely referenced law enforcement and instead focused on advocating for legalization. Indeed, the only mention of police in the interview transcripts came from one sex worker disclosing that she was married to a police officer. Instead, the Nevada sex workers focused on how regulation and legalization of their sex work made them feel safe, as Angela shared, "I assumed that if there was a regulated industry, things were going to be safe and clean and well run."

Several participants discussed how they publicly advocate for legalized sex work. Andie was a clear leader among the local sex workers in advocating for continuing and expanding the legality of sex work in the US:

> If you criminalize something—that doesn't work! How do you fix it? Legalizing it. Legalizing it looks like what we have here. So I'm gonna fight tooth and nail to keep what we have. So this way we can bring it to the rest of the country. We have to win at the state level, so we do have the ability to take it elsewhere.

Angela shared, "I've always been, since I was young, kind of an advocate for decriminalization," and she even suggested that she started working at one of the brothels in part because "having some first-hand experience would be a great way to back up my position." The legalization of their work and the sense of safety that many felt came with that legal status contributed to their sense of pride and agency. Nicki noted:

> We're here because we want to be here. And you know, a lot of the girls, they're here because they don't want to go out and work for pimps or whatever or get thrown in jail every time they do illegal prostitution. So this is a safe, clean place. They don't have to be ashamed or anything. As you can see, it's nothing to be ashamed of.

HEALTH CARE EXPERIENCES

The two groups' experiences with health care and health care professionals are incredibly different. Up front, it must be noted that the focus groups were more directly focused on health care issues than the interviews were. Yet, both data sources provide insights into each groups' experiences with health care.

The Nepali FSWs shared many instances of being treated poorly by medical professionals who assumed they were sex workers. Nepal aims to provide universal health care, even as the system has struggled to provide sufficient services for its citizens. The health care system in Nepal relies on public sector, for-profit sector, and nongovernmental organizations (NGOs). There are public sector (central, regional, and district) hospitals; primary care health centers; and a range of clinics. Participants had particularly negative experiences at the public sector hospitals, which were described as the primary source of health care for many.

Focus group #4 was led in a passionate discussion about this concern by P9:

> **P9:** Can we say we do this job [sex worker] when we go for a treatment?
> **P3:** We can't.
> **P4:** We can't speak openly.
> **P7:** We can't speak openly like that.
> **P9:** Now leave that . . . even if we go to check for sexually transmitted diseases. If we say, "I have come to check for HIV" . . . we can say that only if our things are confidential there . . . we can't say that . . . if we go to a general hospital or to another hospital.
> **P7:** We can't.
> **P9:** "I am a sex worker. I am engaged in sex profession . . . I have come to check for the sexually transmitted disease. Please check me." Can we say this directly?
> **All:** Can't. (all together)

Treatment at the hospitals is particularly viewed as problematic, even though it is where FSWs often go first. Stories of being treated differently or even refused treatment in relation to their sex worker identity were shared in each of the focus groups. For example:

> **P1:** If we go to big [important] doctor . . . they humiliate and disgrace us saying, "Chya-chya . . . thu-thu" [spit at us].

Moderator: Have you experienced it or heard?
P7: I have experienced it myself when I went for checkup. . . .
P3: They look at us differently . . .
P4: The way they look at us is different.
P1: Now the doctors are like . . . "This girl is like this type" . . .
Now they mostly treat our uterus right . . . They don't treat other
parts . . . But doctors try to touch other parts as well . . . touch
this . . . touch that . . . Doctors are also like that . . . I was . . .
M: They touched here and there . . .
P2: They will do that when they are suspicious [that we are sex
worker]. (FG4)

Some of the negative experiences were tied to the kinds of questions
the doctors asked that the FSWs did not think was relevant to their treatment.

P4: They used to ask me everything while checking.
P2: Like . . . how many clients do you entertain in a day and
how much do you earn?
P8: How many clients in a day . . .
P2: With how many clients do you stay in a day . . . that type
of . . .
P8: That type of question is asked frequently . . . My friends
wish that such questions shouldn't be asked. (FG1)

Such experiences were discussed as why they often avoided formal health
care. Participant #2 from this group later added: "Everyone says that [they don't
go because] questions are asked." Thus, the negative experience of being asked
to reveal private information about their sex work may deter sex workers from
seeking medical treatment.

These women seemed to understand the dangers of reluctance to get
health-care with P4 powerfully saying, "The disease is spread inside the body of
the shy people." They also shared how they would work together to treat their
own ailments because of shame about facing a medical professional. In one
case, they described cutting open a woman's genital wart themselves, explain-
ing, "We didn't go to a health care facility. . . . It was shameful for her. . . . She
was embarrassed."

On the positive side, some of the FSWs mentioned that new "organizations
are opened now, free HIV testing is done, and sexually transmitted diseases are

checked free. Before there was CAC (Nepal), now we have …, and another called SACTS. I know about many organizations … where HIV and sexually transmitted diseases are tested free of cost … Even if we suspect HIV in some way, there are medicines to check whether we are HIV negative or not. In addition, there are medicines to keep us HIV negative our whole life, right?" (P1/FG1).

These NGOs, which are separate from the public sector hospitals, seem to provide medical care with far less stigmatization than government-run programs:

> **P2:** Now, because of the organization, they [health care providers] do not inquire much, so now when we go for a checkup, they do not ask, "With how many customers did you stay or for how many days … have you been involved in sex [sexually active]?
> **P4:** I feel sad when such questions are asked.
> **P2:** They don't ask that much now. (FG1)

In another focus group, a participant similarly shared an impression that the stigmas in medical care are improving:

> [The doctors] are not rude, rather they tell you have to do this and that, and should take this medicine. In the past, there were doctors who used to get angry when you asked them questions but these days we haven't faced such a situation. (P5/FG2)

These examples show how FSWs' experiences with health care providers are improving overall, even if incrementally.

The transgender FSWs also experienced discrimination in hospital settings, though their descriptions suggested that the most salient stigmatized identity was their transgender identity rather than their sex worker identity. As P3 (FG3) noted:

> The most problems are faced by transgenders. When going for a checkup at the hospital, the doctors ask us about our sexual relations. And sometimes the gender categories are female, male and others only. And if we keep our gender as others, it would be a problem. I tell them that I am transgender, and they refuse to do the checkup. Such has happened to me. The doctors who are understanding do not do so, but there are some

who just tease. Now, all the doctors aren't same. Some are well behaved, some aren't.

The transgender participants also mentioned preferring LBGTQ-focused health service locations. They felt that clinics focused specifically on serving LGBTQ individuals were one of the few places they could disclose their various identities and still get the treatment they needed:

> P4: Many transgenders aren't aware so when such questions arise. They keep their problems to themselves.
> P3: They keep them hidden inside themselves.
> P4: For that, we have this clinic where all [LGBTIQ+] can come freely as there is no other such hospital. (FG3)

As a final positive in their experiences with health care, participants shared stories of how medical reports were sometimes vital in obtaining justice for women they knew who had been beaten and raped. The women might take someone who had been raped to a hospital for evaluation and present the report to police. The primary facilitators for using these doctors' reports to help the sex workers charge perpetrators seemed to be the NGO health and service clinics. The clearest example of this came from their story of a very young girl who was raped:

> That old man raped, who is 60-65 years old, raped her . . . After he raped her, he denied that and said, "No." But after we showed the evidence . . . he couldn't deny that. : . . . The evidence was the doctor's report and after the doctor's report . . . I called Sahara organization (nongovernmental organization) for help and then that girl child was taken to the Sahara organization. . . . I sent her there. . . . He was then sent to jail . . . It's been eight years now. It's been nine years. It's been ten years now . . . and this year only he was out of the jail. (P9/FG4)

The Nevada sex workers have strikingly different experiences with finding and receiving health care. Although these interviews were less focused on health care issues, much can be gleaned from the ways health and health care came up in the interviews. Most brothels have at least part-time on-site doctors for basic medical assistance and regular testing (Blithe and Wolfe 2017). Much of the brothel's motivation for these doctors is to ensure that the women are "medically clear," that is, free of sexually transmitted infections as required by law.

The women are legally required to be tested every seven days. As brothel madam Katie shared: "Medically clear [is] when they—Every seven days they see the doctor for chlamydia, gonorrhea, every STD, HIV, AIDS, all of that, syphilis."

Such access to regular onsite and stigma-free testing sounds like what the Nepali FSWs would like to have. In addition, there is no deliberation over whether to disclose one's status as a sex worker in their health care while they are working. There are, Katie went on to share, however, some restrictions of personal freedom that come with this health care:

> When [the ladies] come here and they've seen the doctor and they're medically clear, then they can no longer just run to town for this or for that. They have to go with a staff like our runner because then if they go on their own, then they're no longer medically clear.

Nevada's brothel-based sex workers serve "contracts." Because legal sex workers are independent contractors, they set their own schedules laid out in these contracts and purchase their own insurance. While contract periods vary, a common contract period is to work two weeks on-site at the brothel and then have two weeks off. Dani, who lives within an hour of the brothel, works a traditional five-day week and travels home on the weekends. Natalie, who travels from out of Nevada to the brothel, works two weeks on and four weeks off. For the duration of this contract period, their actions are highly regulated and supervised via what is sometimes called "lockdown policy."

Furthermore, the legal regulations are such that if a woman continues to engage in sex work after testing positive for HIV, she can be charged with a felony (NRS 201.358), and the brothel owners are liable for resulting damages (NRS 41.1397). Thus, despite the already existing requirement that all sexual activity involves condom use/barrier protection, legal brothel-based sex work is not an option for someone who is HIV positive. On the plus side, according to several sources, no brothel worker has tested positive for HIV since the testing requirement was implemented in 1985 (Greenmore 2017; Weitzer 2012).

Overall, the Nevada workers sometimes mentioned personal interests in mental health, sexual health, and even something called "ancestral health." Several of them framed their sex work as a form of therapy and mental health work for the men they served. As Belle shared:

> They [sex workers] can still feel better about themselves while

> they're involved in it for the therapeutic stuff. They help heal
> broken people. Does it get any better than that? You know,
> they're therapists. So many guys come in, and they have been
> traumatized by a woman.

Two participants shared stories of major health care concerns treated outside of the brothels, but they did not mention any problems in getting treatment on and off contract.

DISCUSSION

In this chapter, we are considering experiences of sex workers in a legalized system (near Reno) and sex workers in an ambiguously and indirectly criminalized system (Kathmandu). The analysis highlights how FSWs working under different legalization/criminalization structures obtain personal and health support, and why and how they conceal or proclaim their sex work identities.

On the one hand, it would be ideal to interview sex workers from very similar cultures such as those from a Nevada city where sex work is still criminalized to compare to interviews with sex workers in Reno's legal brothels. Yet, this project arose more organically than strategically as we brought together two independently collected sets of data. Therefore, we are not arguing for a direct causal relationship between legality and stigma of sex work, but the comparison between two countries with distinct stances on (de)criminalization/legalization of sex work is instructive.

In terms of similarities, both groups fit Ashforth and Kreiner's (1999) definitions of dirty work, and, yet, the discourses around moral taint and necessity of the sex work vary. The Nevada FSWs suggest their work is necessary in several ways, particularly in how often they described themselves as providing a service to men (and women) who face physical and mental hindrances to a fulfilling sex life and intimate relationships. They did not share many instances of being verbally or physically challenged about the morality of their work. In contrast, the Nepali FSWs faced constant moral judgment of even the possibility that they might be engaging in sex work. Such moral taint informs their disclosure decisions.

Both groups also discussed how safety concerns typically guide their disclosure decisions. In Nevada, the women find safety in the legalized structures. They repeatedly referred to the brothels as safe. Specifically, they said they felt safer in them than outside the brothels. However, when engaging with others outside the brothels they may hide their sex worker identities, and they acknowledge the potential for an uncomfortable or potentially harassing situation if they are identified as a sex worker when outside the brothel.

In Nepal, safety is difficult to achieve even for a moment. FSWs perceive threats to their safety: from husbands and wives who might beat them and throw them out of their homes over disclosure; from clients who may steal from them and rape or beat them; from police and neighbors who may chase, beat, or detain them; and from medical professionals who may refuse to treat them. The NGO organizations that provide specialized services (and through which we found participants and conducted focus groups) seem to be one of the very few spaces in which they might feel a modicum of safety.

Both groups also often chose to hide their sex worker identity or keep it distinct from their other identities. The brothel workers use alternative personas and stage names in the brothels that help them achieve some sense of privacy and safety when they leave them. The Nepali FSWs seek to hide their sex work identities constantly. It is worth noting that even in these focus groups, conducted by the fourth author, who works for one of the generally trusted NGOs, there were times where the first author had to check with the third author for assistance in determining if references in the transcripts to other types of work were part of how these women regularly hide and obscure the kind of work they are doing or not.

Nepali participants' stories of struggles for dignity and quality care in health care were heartbreaking. Unfortunately, our focus group data from Nepal aligns with prior studies' reports of sex workers experiencing discrimination in health care settings. For example, in a prior study of sex workers, violence, and HIV in four Asian countries, all the reported instances of discrimination (e.g., doctors denying treatment) and verbal abuse (e.g., being mocked) in the Nepali sample occurred "at government-run health centers and public hospitals" (Bhattacharjya et al. 2015, 79).

In contrast, the Nevada sex workers appeared to have access to onsite health care that did not challenge their sense of dignity and met their needs for care. However, they were not directly asked by the second author about their experiences with disclosing the sex worker identity in health care settings outside of the brothels. Future research should attend more to this issue and concern.

Overall, these two groups of FSWs generate distinct pictures of engaging in prostitution. The culture-based moral stigma in Nepal appears to be so strong that even if the criminalization of the sex work is ambiguous, it is consistently interpreted as work that if not actually illegal, is permissible to treat it as such for the good of the community. It is not recognized as an occupation in Nepal and is still frequently viewed as the same as sex trafficking. Only one of the focus group members directly referenced the idea that sex work should not be as stigmatized as it is. Instead, most of them view their participation in sex work as a shameful necessity.

The Nevada workers tended to be proud of their work, were far more likely to tell their friends and family about the sex work identity, and directly challenged suggestions that they ever feel any shame associated with their work. Their public advocacy for maintaining and expanding legal sex work seemed tied to this pride and desire to change public opinion. In fact, several participants noted how happy they were to talk with the second author and how important they feel it is for people to visit the brothels and see what they are like for themselves.

In summary, this chapter qualitatively compares the experiences of sex workers in legalized and ambiguously criminalized systems. The two groups share a focus on maintaining a sense of safety while engaging in a dirty work occupation, but they differ greatly in why and how they conceal or proclaim their sex work identities and how and where they obtain personal and health support.

REFERENCES

Ashforth, Blake E., and Glen E. Kreiner. "'How Can You Do It?': Dirty Work and the Challenge of Constructing a Positive Identity," *Academy of Management Review* 24, no. 3 (1999): 413–34. https://doi.org/10.5465/amr.1999.2202129.

Ashforth, Blake E., and Glen E. Kreiner. "Dirty Work and Dirtier Work: Differences In Countering Physical, Social, and Moral Stigma," *Management and Organization Review* 10, no. 1 (2014): 81–108. https://doi.org/10.1111/more.12044.

Bekker, Linda-Gail, Leigh Johnson, Frances Cowan, Cheryl Overs, Donela Besada, Sharon Hillier, and Willard Cates, Jr. "Combination HIV Prevention for Female Sex Workers: What is the Evidence?" *The Lancet* 385, no. 9962 (2015): 72–87. https://doi.org/10.1016/S0140-6736(14)60974-0.

Benoit, Cecilia, Michaela Smith, Mikael Jansson, Priscilla Healey, and Douglas Magnuson. "The Relative Quality of Sex Work," *Work, Employment and Society 35*, no. 2 (2021): 239–255. https://doi.org/10.1177/0950017020936872.

Bhattacharjya, Manjima, Emma Fulu, Emma Murthy, Meena Saraswathi Seshu, Julia Cabassi, and Marta Vallejo-Mestres. *The Right(s) Evidence: Sex Work, Violence, and HIV in Asia. A Multi-Country Qualitative Study.* Bangkok: UNFPA and UNDP, 2015.

Blithe, Sarah Jane, and Anna Wiederhold Wolfe. "Work–Life Management in Legal Prostitution: Stigma and Lockdown in Nevada's Brothels," *Human Relations* 70, no. 6 (2017): 725-750. https://doi.org/10.1177%2F0018726716674262

Brents, Barbara, Crystal Jackson, and Kathryn Hausbeck. *The State of Sex: Tourism, Sex and Sin in the New American Heartland.* New York: Routledge, 2009.

Grandy, Gina, and Sharon Mavin. "Emotion Management as Struggle in Dirty Work: The Experiences of Exotic Dancers," *International Journal of Work Organisation and Emotion 6*, no. 2 (2014): 131-154. https://doi.org/10.1504/IJWOE.2014.060927.

Greenmore, Sarah. "I'm a sex worker in a legal brothel—here are the biggest misconceptions about what I do." *The Independent US.* November 12, 2017. https://www.independent.co.uk/voices/comment/i-m-a-sex-worker-in-a-legal-brothel-here-are-the-five-biggest-misconceptions-about-what-i-do-10460454.html

Hughes, Everett C. *Men and Their Work.* California: Free Press, 1958.

Human Trafficking and Transportation (Control) Act, 2007: Its Implementation, Kathmandu: FWLD, 2014.

Lutnick, Alexandra, and Deborah Cohan. "Criminalization, Legalization or Decriminalization Of Sex Work: What Female Sex Workers Say in San Francisco, USA," *Reproductive Health Matters* 17, no. 34 (2009): 38-46. https://doi.org/10.1016/S0968-8080(09)34469-9.

McCarthy, Bill, Cecilia Benoit, Mikael Jansson, and Kat Kolar. "Regulating Sex Work: Heterogeneity In Legal Strategies," *Annual Review of Law and Social Science* 8, no. 1 (2012): 255-271. https://doi.org/10.1146/annurev-lawsocsci-102811-173915.

Miller, Coty R., and Nuria Haltiwanger. "Prostitution and the Legalization/Decriminalization Debate," *Georgetown Journal of Gender and the Law* 5, (2004): 207. https://search-ebscohostcom.proxy.mul.missouri.edu/login.aspx?direct=true&db=edshol&AN=edshol.hein.journals.grggenl5.18&site=eds-live&scope=site.

Nepal Law Commission. "Criminal (Code) Act, 2074." *International Labor Organization.* October 16, 2017. http://www.ilo.org/dyn/natlex/docs/ ELECTRONIC/106060/129899/F1095481449/NPL106060%20Npl.pdf.

Raut, Balram Prasad. "Legislative Approaches to Prostitution: Legalizing or Decriminalizing for Nepal?" *NJA Law Journal* 9 (2015): 187–208. https://search-ebscohost-com.proxy.mul.missouri.edu/login.aspx?direct=true&db=edshol&AN=edshol.hein.journals.njal9.17&site=eds-live&scope=site.

Tanaka, Masako. "Advocating Sex Workers' Rights by Identity-Based Associations in Nepal," *Asian Journal of Law and Society* 7, no. 2 (2020): 265–74. https://doi.org/10.1017/als.2020.11.

Weitzer, Ronald. *Legalizing Prostitution: From Illicit Vice to Lawful Business.* NYU Press, 2012.

Wolfe, Anna Wiederhold, and Sarah Jane Blithe. "Managing Image in a Core-Stigmatized Organization: Concealment and Revelation in Nevada's Legal Brothels," *Management Communication Quarterly* 29, no. 4 (2015): 539-563. https://doi.org/10.1177/0893318915596204.

Chapter 2

Fractured Organizational Support for Sex Workers

Sarah Jane Blithe and Tennley A. Vik

Sex workers around the world continue to experience violence, stigmatization, criminalization, and discrimination. Historically, the horrendous treatment of sex workers has been pushed into the shadows, disregarded, and accepted as part of the occupation. However, a growing social movement to support sex workers has moved into mainstream discourse and policy. Advocacy groups and political hopefuls have publically demanded an end to violence, criminalization, and discrimination for sex workers. Despite the progress that has occurred, support for sex workers is dispersed across a myriad of collectives with differing agendas and disparate views of support.

In what Crystal Jackson calls a "framing battle"[1] over the meaning of sex work, victimization, protection, and support, sex workers, their allies, and their opposition have pushed different versions of organizational support. From rescue organizations to failed labor unions, the demand for support organizations remains unfulfilled while the organizations designed to provide support flounder in their division. It is complicated to study sex work support organizations because they take multiple forms and carry disparate views on support. Some of these organizations are nonprofits; others are for profit. Some are social networks, informal collectives, or coalitions. Some organizations are rescue organizations, mutual aid, or governmental agencies. Others still are labor rights or health advocacy organizations. More still are hybrids of these forms. As such, it can be difficult to identify the organizational role in providing support and impossible to study support organizations and their practices as a cohesive whole. Studying the efforts of sex worker support organizations can reveal a lot about societal perspectives on sex work and how it is situated in the broader cultural and political context in which policies will develop.[2]

In this chapter, we analyze the connection between organizational messaging directed at sex workers and social support. We begin by situating the study in literature about sex work stigma and social support. Following, we outline the major differing perspectives guiding sex worker support organizations: abolitionists, sex workers' rights, and health care, in which we highlight the types of organizations offering support in each area. Ultimately, we argue that there is insufficient organizational support for sex workers, and that the polarization of supportive organizations for sex workers hinders sex workers from accessing necessary support.

A COMPLICATED CONTEXT OF STIGMA

Sex workers are steeped in stigma. Sex worker stigma is wildly disproportionate to the experience of people with other occupations[3]—even those who are in stigmatized professions (such as garbage collectors, for example). Dirty work[4] refers to occupations that are seen as disgusting or are otherwise degraded and stigmatized by others because the work is physically, morally, or socially objectionable by the larger segment of society. People working in dirty work jobs or industries often experience severe stigma related to their work and can be marginalized in society. Ashforth and Kreiner expanded on the conceptualization of taint in dirty work.[5] They explained physical taint as working with garbage, death, pollution, or waste (such as embalmers); or occupations that are particularly dangerous (such as soldiers). Moral taint occurs when an activity is viewed as sinful or dubious (such as professional gamblers). Social taint is conferred when workers have regular contact with stigmatized groups (such as prison guards).[6] Sex workers experience all of these forms of dirty work taint,[7] as well as emotional taint—stigma related to work that requires high levels of emotional display.[8] Bowen and Bungay (2016) argued that sex workers experience symbolic stigma,[9] in that they are deemed as a health threat to society. They also experience whore stigma[10] because they sell intimacy for money. In short, sex workers experience layers of stigma and taint related to their occupations.

Stigma can be deeply damaging to sex workers. Some sex workers have reported that they have a difficult time engaging in everyday activities such as volunteering, banking, getting loans, and paying taxes. They have also reported difficulty in gaining employment outside of sex work, if and when they decide to switch careers.[11] The stigma around sex work can make it difficult to form healthy romantic relationships. Much of the trouble is related to occupational identity—through which workers experience deeply personal attachments with work. In the United States, occupational identities are so important to the understanding of the self and others that people regularly ask, "What do you do?" as a way to understand what type of person they have encountered.[12] Occupational selves develop early in individuals, and shape not only economic parameters of life, but also specific languages, skills, or values.[13] Because occupations define individuals so acutely, stigma that is leveled at one's choice of work can be particularly difficult to bear. It is akin to stigma leveled directly at the self.

In addition to the repeated hurts and discomforts existing in everyday life, sex workers are also disproportionally exposed to sexual violence, physical violence, and murder, particularly those who work outdoors, sex workers of color, migrant sex workers, and transgender sex workers.[14] This violence comes from a variety of sources including general street violence, violence by clients or people posing as clients, and police.[15] Macro discourses about sex workers serve to dehumanize and objectify women so much so that the physical harm sex workers experience is often overlooked. There is a clear need to reform such negative stereotypes and narratives, so that sex workers can experience a more positive well-being and greater safety.[16]

Taken all together, the stigma and risk for violence suggest that sex workers are a vulnerable population in need of stronger social support. A number of organizations play (or should play) an important role in providing such support. However, to date there is an unacceptable lack in sufficient organizational or institutional support for sex workers.

SOCIAL SUPPORT IN ORGANIZATIONS

When examining organizations, it is important to remember the turn in organizational communication that places *people at the center of focus* within organizations. Specifically, we privilege the voices of the people within organizations, or in this circumstance the voices of the people that the organizations are trying to help. This theoretical turn in organizational communication is best thought of as a post Weick model.[17] We are particularly interested in privileging the perspectives of sex workers because they are the central focus of how the communication is affecting others.[18] We understand these organizations as centers of social justice that both enable and constrain sex workers and the discourses surrounding sex work. As we continue to wrestle with how sex workers interpret the messages from organizations, we center the perspectives of sex workers and their perspectives on social support.

Social support is a complex communicative phenomenon that has been studied in a plethora of ways, primarily in dyadic communication. One of the most encompassing definitions of social support is simply, "knowing what to say (as well as what not to say)."[19] Of course there are multiple theoretical understandings of what social support is, how to measure/code social support, and where the focus of the social support should be (on the sender or on the receiver of the social support). One of the most helpful theoretical frames for social support is person-centered messages. These messages are focused on the individual in need of support (receiver), rather than the person providing support (sender). To better understand how support is enacted, we must examine the messages constructed by the sender (in this case an organization) and how those messages are, in turn, perceived and understood by the receiver (in this case sex workers). This theory constitutes supportive messages in a dichotomous frame; specifically, low person-centered messages (not as supportive) and high person-centered messages (as supportive).

Burleson defines high person-centered messages as "comforting messages explicitly recognize and legitimize the other's feelings, help the other to articulate those feelings, elaborate reasons why those feelings might be felt, and assist the other to see how those feelings fit in a broader context."[20] In other words, high person-centered messages place a focus on the individual needing support and center their emotions and feelings. On the opposite side of the dichotomy are low person-centered messages, defined as messages that "deny the other's feelings and perspective by criticizing his or her feelings, challenging the legitimacy of those feelings, or telling the other how he or she should act and feel."[21] Low person-centered messages question the validity of the feelings of the person in need of support and require far less communicative skill to construct than high person-centered messages. Although a person constructing a social support message may perceive that their message is meant to make the other person feel better, because of the communicative skill, time, and energy needed to construct high person-centered messages, people often default to less supportive communication. When a person receives consistent low person-centered messages, they may develop negative health outcomes, including mental health struggles.[22]

As previously mentioned, social support varies from person to person,[23] across situations,[24] and is likely to increase over the lifetime. "It appears that when a person has honed their communicative skill in social support, their interpersonal relationships (romantic, family, friendship, social/work relationships) are able to be maintained."[25] In other words, social support formulates the foundation for engaging in communicative behaviors that make people feel validated in their interpersonal relationships, and subsequently make our interpersonal relationships happier and more successful. It seems as if social support should be readily expressed in all interpersonal relationships, however, social support can be withheld for a number of reasons including incessant talk of a problem,[26] lack of communication skill,[27] lack of resources (both tangible and physical),[28] and exhaustion/burn out.[29] Communication messages perceived as supportive (i.e., high person-centered messages) are critical to creating and maintaining healthy interpersonal relationships.[30]

We know that interpersonal communication is an ongoing process[31] and should be studied as such. However, it is difficult to study social support in ongoing, long-term circumstances. For this chapter, we aim to understand how organizations posit social support messages to sex workers and how these messages are interpreted by sex workers. Although this might seem like a static moment in time, sex workers are bombarded by communicative messages from organizations. We argue that all of these messages are providing social support, but as we previously discussed *effective* social support hinges on the perception of the individual receiving the support, and these messages can vary drastically in terms of the construction of the social support message.

Fractured Theories of Support

As mentioned, sex worker support organizations are quite divided in how they view prostitution and support. Two enduring perspectives tend to guide how organizations view sex work and thus shape the type of support they provide. In this section, we examine abolition, sex workers' rights, and health care perspectives, including some key organizations associated with each.

ABOLITION
Organizations that take an abolitionist stance toward sex work offer a particular

version of support for sex workers that reflects their definition of sex work itself.[32] Because abolitionist advocates believe that all sex work is violence, domination, and exploitation, most organizations offering support for sex workers in this tradition are "rescue"[33] organizations that try to help women out of sex work. They also provide an array of other services, such as counseling, temporary housing, and legal help. Rescue organizations are a diverse group of government agencies, nonprofits, collaborative networks, social workers, law enforcement, and researchers.[34] This particular brand of support organization assumes that all sex workers want to get out of the industry and tend to conflate sex work with sexual slavery, sex trafficking, and domestic violence.[35] They cast sex workers as victims or survivors.

Prohibition advocates have been remarkably successful, and have drawn what Weitzer calls a "moral panic" about sex work. High-profile advocates such as Catharine MacKinnon and Melissa Farley use dramatic language and extreme examples to organize for the complete abolition of sex work. These organizations assume that sex workers were trafficked, forced into their occupations by pimps, were tricked, drugged, or abused.[36] Prohibition organizations stand firm against the legalization of prostitution and generally make similar claims:

- Legal prostitution is a root cause of sex trafficking.
- Prostitution increases violence and exploitation of women and children.
- Legal prostitution leads to a growth of illegal sex work.
- Sex work is always exploitative.[37]

A multitude of organizations take this approach across the globe. For example, Eaves' Poppy Project in the United Kingdom provides "support, advocacy and accommodation to trafficked women; that is, women who have been brought into England or Wales to be exploited in some way."[38] The goal of Farley's organization in San Francisco, California, Prostitution Research and Education (PRE), is to "abolish the institution of prostitution while at the same time advocating for alternatives to trafficking and prostitution—including emotional and physical health care for women in prostitution."[39]

Awaken (in Reno, Nevada) explains its mission is "to transform our community with the ultimate goal of eradicating commercial sexual exploitation. We aim for victims of commercial sexual exploitation to be restored to their fullest potential."[40] Awaken's main goal is to completely eliminate sex work, and advocacy toward that goal is part of its support. In a similar way, the Chicago Alliance Against Sexual Exploitation in Illinois claims to envision "a community free from all forms of sexual exploitation, including sexual assault and the commercial sex trade . . . CAASE addresses the culture, institutions, and individuals that perpetrate, profit from, or support sexual exploitation."[41] CAASE also promotes the complete elimination of sex work and views all forms of sex work as exploitative.

SEX WORKERS' RIGHTS

Sex workers' rights groups support sex workers in achieving legitimacy in their occupational choice. These groups aim to include sex workers in conversations about sex work and what sex workers need.[42] In general, sex workers' rights organizations believe:

- Consensual sex work is different from trafficking.
- Many sex workers choose their occupation freely and enjoy their work.
- Sex work is legitimate work.
- Sex work is not always oppressive.
- Many sex workers are empowered and are not victims.
- Sex workers have the right to work safely, free from arrest, violence, police harassment, and stigma.
- Sex work should be decriminalized.

As Jackson described, sex workers' rights organizations want sex workers to have "the right to work safely—free from arrest, police harassment, and violence; free to report violence or theft; free to remain as a primary caretaker for a child/children."[43] Like abolitionist groups, sex workers' rights collectives also provide legal services, therapy, health services, research, events, networking, support, and advocacy.

Global and local efforts have resulted in a multitude of organizations. At the international level, the Global Network of Sex Work Projects (NSWP) represents ninety-nine countries in its efforts to amplify "the voices of sex worker-led organizations advocating for rights-based services."[44] The NSWP has been involved in international policy development, constantly advocating for language that recognizes sex work as work in international policies and protocols. The Red Umbrella Fund is a "global grant-making mechanism for, and by, sex workers"[45] that develops the grant-making capacities of sex worker leaders and conducts funding advocacy.

Many more support organizations exist at the regional and national levels. Sex workers' rights groups began organizing in Europe in the mid 1970s.[46] Many of the world's strongest sex work advocacy organizations originate from this region. However there are strong organizations around the world. For example, the Scarlet Alliance in Australia, the Sex Workers Education and Advocacy Taskforce (SWEAT) in South Africa, the Asia Pacific Network of Sex Workers (APNSW) in Asia, the Durbar Mahila Samanwaya Committee in India, and the Red de Mujeres Trabajadoras Sexuales de Latinoamérica y el Caribe (RedTraSex) in Latin America and the Caribbean are all major regional sex workers' rights organizations.

The development of successful sex workers' rights organizations have been slower to develop in the United States. COYOTE (Call Off Your Old Tired Ethics) has multiple local chapters in the US that "work for the repeal of the prostitution laws and an end to the stigma associated with sexual work."[47] However, most local chapters are fairly inactive and claim they will organize together when necessary to advocate for a particular issue. In a similar way, the Desiree Alliance scheduled conferences and events to "advocate sex workers' human, health, labor, and civil rights . . . [and] for the full anti-criminalization of sex work."[48] Although the organization still exists, it is not holding events or conferences because it perceives the current climate in the United States too dangerous for sex workers to be public about their identities.[49] Madame Bella Cummins' Onesta Foundation seeks "to provide awareness and advocacy for a fun, safe, healthy, and transparent adult sensual services industry in the great state of Nevada and to promote legalization across the United States and the World!"[50] However, the organization has had a difficult time growing because perceptions about laws and brothel rules prohibit sex workers from working with or even socializing with sex workers from competing brothels.

SEX WORKER HEALTH ORGANIZATIONS

Health advocacy groups make up a third pillar of sex work support organizations. These organizations support sex workers in health-related ways. They include community-based "street" organizations; large medical non-profit and for-profit organizations; and governmental organizations. Most of these support organizations assume that adequate health care is difficult to find for sex workers, and that stigma infiltrates sex workers' abilities to access health care. The basic claims and assumptions of sex work health advocacy groups are:

- Sex workers have high rates of STIs, particularly HIV.[51]
- Sex workers experience a high rate of violence.[52]
- Sex workers lack sufficient health care.
- Sex workers often require substance abuse treatment.
- Health care providers demonstrate stigma toward sex workers.
- Sex workers are a threat to public health.

Health-based support organizations often strategize how to get sex workers adequate treatment and care. They advocate for protective policies, adequate housing, and destigmatized access to broad health care. Popular goals for this group are increased condom use and STI awareness campaigns; testing services; and administering antiretroviral therapy.[53] Most of these organizations explicitly claim that stigma is the root cause of the inferior health care that sex workers receive.

Sex worker health organizations are both global and local. The World Health Organization (WHO) reaches billions of individuals each year. Although its scope is broad, the WHO focuses on the health of sex workers, specifically in HIV prevention and treatment. Sex workers are often recipients of WHO directives, and the WHO publishes research about sex worker health (again, primarily about HIV and other STIs) every couple of months. Yale University's Global Health Justice Partnership (GHJP) promotes its role in "protecting the Health and Rights of Sex Workers in the US and globally."[54] This group advocates for sex workers by implementing health-related programs and by interrogating policies and programs that could be important to sex workers (such as safe harbor laws).

While the WHO and the GHJP put forth great effort to prevent and treat STIs, some organizations take a more holistic approach to sex worker health care. St. James Infirmary in San Francisco, California, focuses on the health and safety of sex workers. It offers a free health clinic, STI testing, mental health support and counseling, and hormone replacement therapy for transgender clients. It also keeps a list of "bad dates," individuals who have acted violently or inappropriately toward sex workers. St. James Infirmary is run "by Sex Workers for Sex Workers."[55] St. James Infirmary is different than other health-focused sex worker support organizations. It clearly prioritizes the holistic health and well-being of individual sex workers and provides tailored support.

Discussion

Globally, the abolitionist paradigm has been remarkably successful and has shaped policies and public perceptions around the world. Spin-off rescue organizations and anti-trafficking organizations attract high-profile spokespeople and extensive funding. Health care organizations have also been quite successful in securing funding and are perhaps the most successful in their missions around the world. Sex workers' rights organizations, however, have not yet found mainstream success. While there are successful organizations, they tend to be more local and less effective in providing support. Part of the problem for sex workers' rights organizations is that abolitionist groups extend negative messaging directly attacking the sex workers' rights perspective. Sex workers' rights organizations also promote messaging that goes against all the missions of abolitionist organizations. While the organizations are having a tug-of-war in their perspectives, it eclipses the opportunity for sex workers to obtain the kind of support they need. Instead of playing rhetorical games about whether or not sex work is legitimate work or always exploitative, organizations that set out to support sex workers should busy themselves in providing support. Splintering support based on differing ideologies makes distributing social support less effective and allows sex work stigma to fester and grow. Moving forward, organizations should focus on social support strategies rather than attempting to push their particular ideologies.

We posit that organizations providing messages of social support that embrace sex work as legitimate work are providing high person-centered messages. These messages provide sex workers with social support that places *their needs and desires at the center* of the communicative message, and may have positive health impacts, including improved mental health for sex workers. On the opposite end of the spectrum are organizations that posit that all sex work is removing agency from the sex worker and that all women engaging in sex work are being trafficked. While this may seem like a supportive message to get women out of sex work, we resist this claim. Instead, we offer that these messages are low person-centered messages that do not focus the message on the needs of the sex workers.

Essentially, organizations are giving more nuanced (and better) social support when they focus their messages on sex work as legitimate work rather than a point of intervention. High person-centered messages center sex workers, providing them with agency, which places the message of support *on the person needing support*. A juxtaposition exists here, where low person-centered messages are provided by organizations to help get sex workers out of sex work. However, those organizations make a false assumption that all sex workers need to/want to get out of sex work. When met with low person-centered messages, sex workers may see an increase in negative health outcomes, including poor mental health. These implications have lasting impacts for sex workers. Although there are sex workers who are trafficked and need assistance, focusing communicative messages on all sex workers negates agency of sex workers and may cause lasting negative impacts.

There is an unspoken expectation in society that other people will provide societal support.[56] However, the skill and nuance required for positive social support are critically important for the way the recipient experiences it. Social support messages can be constructed by other people, or in this case, by organizations. The social support messages we are referencing are not manufactured independent of people; they are instead constructed by people in the organization with a specific purpose. These messages are constructed and reconstructed by organizations to fit the mission and needs of the organization. These iterative messages are received by sex workers on a daily basis through social media, online platforms, interactions with clients, and interactions with family and friends. These messages that are produced by organizations are reinforced through interpersonal interactions and also bombard sex workers. The prolific nature of these messages makes sex workers more susceptible to them, and thus makes the messages incredibly influential. This pattern is of particular importance because sex workers may not be receiving many messages that provide them with ample support, which likely reinforces negative health outcomes and implications. While these implications may seem small, these discourses are also interpreted by people who do not engage in sex work, which may perpetuate violence against sex workers.

THEORETICAL CONTRIBUTIONS

We suggest that organizational messaging should be examined specifically for social support and understood in a dichotomous way (i.e., examining messages for person-centered messages). People in organizations who distribute messages should consider those that give agency to sex workers, which will likely be better received and provide more social support. It is important to reflect on the ideological differences in these organizations; for example, some organizations simply want to assist sex workers in exiting the organization. However, we suggest that these messages are not helpful and actually are quite hurtful to many sex workers who view their work as a legitimate form of work. Although there may be ways to reformulate low person-centered messages into high person-centered messages[57], this may take significant reflection and work by the organizations to provide more social support to sex workers.

We suggest that researchers empirically examine messaging from organizations, understanding that social support is a dynamic and constitutive communicative practice. In other words, social support is an ongoing communicative process, and these messages give meaning to organizations. It is important to note that these organizations do have *good intentions*, at least in their own perspective, but that the messaging that is constructed that does not give agency to sex workers is problematic and harmful.

This manuscript provides a rich theoretical contribution to our understanding of how social support, organizational communication, and stigma work together to affect messaging received by sex workers. Specifically, organizations construct messages that are supposed to provide social support. These types of messages are dichotomized into two forms of social support: 1) low person-centered messages/low social support, and 2) high person-centered messages/high social support.[58] We believe that organizations providing messages emphasizing exit from sex work are providing low person-centered messages, which are problematic. Instead, organizations that are providing social support that focuses on the individual and sex work as legitimate work are providing messages that will be received by sex workers as helpful and supportive. This is especially important because sex workers are bombarded with stigma, and low person-centered messages seem to increase stigma, while high person-centered messages decrease stigma. This is of particular interest because sex workers are bombarded with communicative decisions daily. If sex workers perceive that they are supported, they may be more likely to accept help from the organizations in question and are more likely to engage in disclosure to other people in their lives.[59] These disclosures are particularly important because of the ongoing nature of communication, and the fact that sex workers need social support (as we all do) from those around us, as well as organizations that influence our everyday lives.

PRACTICAL CONTRIBUTIONS

A number of practical contributions emerged from this research. First, organizations with goals of supporting sex workers must analyze their perspective about sex work to avoid reifying stereotypical narratives about sex workers. Supporting organizations have such drastically different versions of support, and an organizational analysis of the type of support offered is important. It is likely that available support aligns with the organizational leaders' perspectives on sex work itself, which can leave some individuals without the kind of support they need. In general, we recommend that supportive organizations have a reckoning with some divergent perspectives of sex work. If the goal of these organizations is truly about providing support, then support should be at the forefront of their efforts, rather than campaigning.

This research also provides an opportunity to think more about labor unions and employee/independent contractor statuses for/of sex workers. Sex work is legal in some geographical locations, and yet sex workers do not experience the same organizational support that people in other stigmatized occupations experience. It is possible that sex workers could have a labor union to support them.

Finally, it is necessary to involve and promote actual sex workers or former sex workers into positions of power in support organizations. Too many organizations that claim to support sex workers are run by people outside the industry. We are not arguing that these organizations must be made up exclusively of sex workers. However, stigma and power have pushed sex work organizing away from the people closest to the work. When anti-sex work organizers or brothel owners are the main organizers *and* the primary beneficiaries of organizational support, the purpose of the organization cannot be achieved. Put simply: sex workers must be part of the organizational support solutions.

To conclude, we argue that organizations that seek to support sex workers must push beyond divisive ideologies about the legitimacy of sex work. Instead, organizations should champion agency in their campaigns, organizational messaging, and support of sex workers. Sex workers need to be agents within these organizations and have a pivotal role in how the organizations choose to "help." In partnering with sex workers, organizations have the opportunity to learn how people working in sex work occupations experience these messages. Organizations must take the time to construct more communicatively complex support messages that place sex workers (rather than organizational exit) at the center of their mission and actions as an organization. We understand that these goals are lofty and ask that organizations rethink their role and their dialogue with sex workers. We champion the rights, agency, and perceptions of sex workers, and encourage organizations that seek to support sex workers to analyze their conceptions and strategies of support.

REFERENCES

Agustín, Laura María. Sex at the Margins: Migration, Labour Markets and the Rescue Industry. Bloomsbury Publishing, 2008.

Armstrong, Lynzi. "Stigma, decriminalisation, and violence against street-based sex workers: Changing the narrative." Sexualities 22, no. 7-8 (2019): 1288-1308.

Ashforth, Blake E., and Glen E. Kreiner. "'How can you do it?': Dirty work and the challenge of constructing a positive identity." Academy of Management Review 24, no. 3 (1999): 413-434.

Ashforth, Blake E., and Glen E. Kreiner. "Dirty work and dirtier work: Differences in countering physical, social, and moral stigma." Management and Organization Review 10, no. 1 (2014): 81-108.

Blithe, Sarah Jane. *Gender Equality and Work–Life Balance: Glass Handcuffs and Working Men in the US*. CRC Press, 2018.

Blithe, Sarah Jane, Anna Wiederhold Wolfe, and Breanna Mohr. *Sex and Stigma: Stories of Everyday Life in Nevada's Legal Brothels*. NYU Press, 2019.

Bowen, Raven, and Vicky Bungay. "Taint: An examination of the lived experiences of stigma and its lingering effects for eight sex industry experts." *Culture, Health & Sexuality* 18, no. 2 (2016): 184-197.

Burleson, Brant R. "What counts as effective emotional support? Explorations of individual and situational differences." *Studies in Applied Interpersonal Communication* (2008): 207-227.

Burleson, Brant R. "The development of comforting communication skills in childhood and adolescence." *Child Development* (1982): 1578-1588.

Burleson, Brant R. "Age, social-cognitive development, and the use of comforting strategies." *Communications Monographs* 51, no. 2 (1984): 140-153.

Burleson, Brant R. "Emotional support skills." (2003).

Chicago Alliance Against Sexual Violence (CAASE), "About Us." accessed October 11, 2021. https://www.caase.org/mission/.

Cunningham, Stewart, and Sanders, Teela, "Urban justice center sex workers project." July 2017, *The Use of Sex Worker Homicide Statistics in Campaigning*, London School of Hygiene & Tropical Medicine.

Ditmore, Melissa. "Conclusion: Pushing Boundaries in Sex Worker Activism and Research." *Sex Work Matters: Exploring Money, Power and Intimacy in the Sex Industry* (2010): 239-242.

Duck, Steve. "Relationships as unfinished business: Out of the frying pan and into the 1990s." *Journal of Social and Personal Relationships* 7, no. 1 (1990): 5-28.

"Eaves' Poppy 'Project." Eaves. Putting women first, accessed October 11, 2021. https://www.eavesforwomen.org.uk/about-eaves/our-projects/the-poppy-project/

"#GivingTuesday2021 Support Sex Worker Health and Safety." St. James Infirmary, accessed October 11, 2021. https://www.stjamesinfirmary.org

"Global Health Justice Partnership." Yale Law School, accessed October 11, 2021 https://law.

yale.edu/ghjp/projects/gender-sexuality-and-rights/protecting-health-and-rights-sex-workers-us-and-globally

Greene, R. L., Jackson, J. S., Neighbors, H. W. "Mental health and help-seeking behavior." In *Aging in Black America*, eds. J. S. Jackson, L. M. Chatters, & R. J. (Taylor Newbury Park, CA: Sage, 1993), 185–200.

Herek, Gregory M., Keith F. Widaman, and John P. Capitanio. "When sex equals AIDS: Symbolic stigma and heterosexual adults' inaccurate beliefs about sexual transmission of AIDS." *Social Problems* 52, no. 1 (2005): 15-37.

Hughes, Everett Cherrington. "Work and the self." (1951).

Jackson, Crystal A. "Sex Worker Rights Organizing as Social Movement Unionism: Responding to the Criminalization of Work." (2013).

Jackson, Crystal A. "Framing sex worker rights: How US sex worker rights activists perceive and respond to mainstream anti–sex trafficking advocacy." *Sociological Perspectives* 59, no. 1 (2016): 27-45.

Kempadoo, Kamala, and Jo Doezema, eds. *Global Sex Workers: Rights, Resistance, and Redefinition*. Routledge, 2018.

Kuhn, Timothy, Annis G. Golden, Jane Jorgenson, Patrice M. Buzzanell, Brenda L. Berkelaar, Lorraine G. Kisselburgh, Sharon Kleinman, and Disraelly Cruz. "Cultural discourses and discursive resources for meaning/ful work: Constructing and disrupting identities in contemporary capitalism." *Management Communication Quarterly* 22, no. 1 (2008): 162-171.

Makhakhe, Nosipho Faith, Anna Meyer-Weitz, Helen Struthers, and James McIntyre. "The role of health and advocacy organizations in assisting female sex workers to gain access to health care in South Africa." *BMC Health Services Research* 19, no. 1 (2019): 1-9.

McMurray, Robert, and Jenna Ward. "'Why would you want to do that?': Defining emotional dirty work." *Human Relations* 67, no. 9 (2014): 1123-1143.

Minichiello, Victor, John Scott, and Denton Callander. "A new public health context to understand male sex work." *BMC Public Health* 15, no. 1 (2015): 1-11.

"Our movement makes an impact" Dressember. Awaken nonprofit organization, Nevada, accessed October 11, 2021. https://www.dressember.org/impact.

Pheterson, Gail. "The whore stigma: Female dishonor and male unworthiness." *Social Text* 37 (1993): 39-64.

Platt, Lucy, Pippa Grenfell, Rebecca Meiksin, Jocelyn Elmes, Susan G. Sherman, Teela Sanders, Peninah Mwangi, and Anna-Louise Crago. "Associations between sex work laws and sex workers' health: A systematic review and meta-analysis of quantitative and qualitative studies." *PLoS medicine* 15, no. 12 (2018): e1002680.

Stroebe, Wolfgang, Emmanuelle Zech, Margaret S. Stroebe, and Georgios Abakoumkin. "Does social support help in bereavement?" *Journal of Social and Clinical Psychology* 24, no. 7 (2005): 1030-1050.

"Sexual violence against sex workers: fact sheet." Urban Justice Center Sex Workers Project, accessed October 11, 2021. https://swp.urbanjustice.org/news-room/resources

Vik, Tennley A., and Jocelyn M. DeGroot. "I don't let everyone see my struggles: Mothers' social support and privacy management." *Personal Relationships* (2021).

Weick, Karl E. "The social psychology of organizing." *Management* 18, no. 2 (2015): 189.

Weick, Karl E. "Sources of order in underorganized systems: Themes in recent organizational theory." *Organizational Theory and Inquiry* (1985): 106-136.

Weick, Karl E. "Enacted sensemaking in crisis situations [1]." *Journal of Management Studies* 25, no. 4 (1988): 305-317.

Weick, Karl E. "Organized improvisation: 20 years of organizing." *Communication Studies* 40, no. 4 (1989): 241-248.

Weick, Karl E. "The social psychology of organizing." *Management* 18, no. 2 (2015): 189.

Weick, Karl E., and Larry D. Browning. "Argument and narration in organizational communication." *Journal of Management* 12, no. 2 (1986): 243-259.

Weitzer, Ronald. "The mythology of prostitution: Advocacy research and public policy." *Sexuality Research and Social Policy* 7, no. 1 (2010): 15-29.

NOTES

1 Jackson, Crystal A. "Sex Worker Rights Organizing as Social Movement Unionism: Responding to the Criminalization of Work." (2013).

2 Jackson, "Sex Worker Rights."

3 Bowen, Raven, and Vicky Bungay. "Taint: An examination of the lived experiences of stigma and its lingering effects for eight sex industry experts." *Culture, Health & Sexuality* 18, no. 2 (2016): 184-197.

4 Hughes, Everett Cherrington. "Work and the self." (1951).

5 Ashforth, Blake E., and Glen E. Kreiner. "How can you do it?: Dirty work and the challenge of constructing a positive identity." *Academy of Management Review* 24, no. 3 (1999): 413-434.

6 Ashforth and Kreiner, "How Can You Do It?"

7 Ashforth, Blake E., and Glen E. Kreiner. "Dirty work and dirtier work: Differences in countering physical, social, and moral stigma." *Management and Organization Review* 10, no. 1 (2014): 81-108; Blithe, Sarah Jane, Anna Wiederhold Wolfe, and Breanna Mohr. *Sex and Stigma: Stories of Everyday Life in Nevada's Legal Brothels*. NYU Press, 2019.

8 McMurray, Robert, and Jenna Ward. "'Why would you want to do that?': Defining emotional dirty work." *Human Relations* 67, no. 9 (2014): 1123-1143.

9 Herek, G. M., K. F. Widaman, and J. P. Capitanio. 2005. "When sex equals AIDS: Symbolic stigma and heterosexual adults' inaccurate beliefs about sexual transmission of AIDS." *Social Problems* 52 (1): 15–37.

10 Pheterson, g. 1993. "The whore stigma: Female dishonor and male unworthiness." *Social Text* 37: 39–64.

11 Blithe et al., *Sex and Stigma*

12 Sarah Jane Blithe. 2015. *Gender Equality and Work-Life Balance: Glass Handcuffs and Working Men in the U.S.* Routledge.

13 Kuhn, T., Golden, A., Jorgenson, J., Buzzanell, P., Kisselburgh, L., Kleinman, S., and Cruz, D. (2008). Cultural discourses and discursive resources for meaning/ful work: Constructing and disrupting identities in contemporary capitalism. *Management Communication Quarterly*, 22, 162–171. doi:10.1177/0893318908318262.

14 Urban Justice Center Sex Workers Project, "Sexual violence against sex workers: fact sheet," ttps://swp.urbanjustice.org/news-room/resources/, accessed October 11, 2021; Ditmore, Melissa. 2010. "Conclusion: Pushing boundaries in sex worker activism and research," 239-242 in *Sex Work Matters: Exploring Money, Power and Intimacy in the Sex Industry*, edited by M. Ditmore, A. Levy, and A. Willman. London: Zed Books.

15 Urban Justice Center Sex Workers Project; Stewart Cunningham and Teela Sanders, July 2017, The Use of Sex Worker Homicide Statistics in Campaigning, London School of Hygieme & Tropical Medicine.

16 Armstrong, Lynzi. "Stigma, decriminalization, and violence against street-based sex workers: Changing the narrative." *Sexualities* 22, no. 7-8 (2019): 1288-1308.

17 Karl E. Weick "The social psychology of organizing." *Management* 18, no. 2 (2015): 189; Karl E. Weick "Sources of order in underorganized systems: Themes in recent organizational theory." *Organizational theory and inquiry* (1985): 106-136; Karl E. Weick "Enacted sensemaking in crisis situations [1]." *Journal of management studies* 25, no. 4 (1988): 305-317; Karl E. Weick "Organized improvisation: 20 years of organizing." *Communication Studies* 40, no. 4 (1989): 241-248; Karl E. Weick, and Larry D. Browning. "Argument and narration in organizational communication." *Journal of Management* 12, no. 2 (1986): 243-259.

18 Karl E. Weick, and Larry D. Browning. "Argument and narration in organizational communication." *Journal of Management* 12, no. 2 (1986): 243-259.

19 Brant R. Burleson "What counts as effective emotional support? Explorations of individual and situational differences." *Studies in Applied Interpersonal Communication* (2008): 207-227. (p. 208).

20 Burleson "What Counts as Effective."

21 Burleson "What Counts as Effective."

22 Burleson "What Counts as Effective."

23 Brant R. Burleson. "The development of comforting communication skills in childhood and adolescence." *Child Development* (1982): 1578-1588.

24 Brant R. Burleson "Age, social-cognitive development, and the use of comforting strategies." *Communications Monographs* 51, no. 2 (1984): 140-153.

25 Tennley A. Vik, and Jocelyn M. DeGroot. "I don't let everyone see my struggles: Mothers' social support and privacy management." *Personal Relationships* (2021).

26 Wolfgang Stroebe, Emmanuelle Zech, Margaret S. Stroebe, and Georgios Abakoumkin. "Does social support help in bereavement?" *Journal of social and Clinical Psychology* 24, no. 7 (2005): 1030-1050.

27 Burleson "What Counts as Effective."

28 R. L. Greene, Jackson, J. S., Neighbors, H. W. "Mental health and help-seeking behavior." In *Aging in Black America*, eds. J. S. Jackson, L. M. Chatters, & R. J. (Taylor Newbury Park, CA: Sage, 1993), 185–200.

29 Tennley A. Vik, and Jocelyn M. DeGroot. "I don't let everyone see my struggles: Mothers' social support and privacy management." *Personal Relationships* (2021).

30 Brant R. Burleson "Emotional support skills." (2003).

31 Steve Duck. "Relationships as unfinished business: Out of the frying pan and into the 1990s." *Journal of Social and Personal Relationships* 7, no. 1 (1990): 5-28.

32 Weitzer, Ronald. "The mythology of prostitution: Advocacy research and public policy." *Sexuality Research and Social Policy* 7, no. 1 (2010): 15-29.

33 Agustín, Laura María. 2007. *Sex at the Margins: Migration, Labour Markets and the Rescue Industry.* New York and London: Zed Books.

34 Jackson, Crystal A. "Framing sex worker rights: How US sex worker rights activists perceive and respond to mainstream anti–sex trafficking advocacy." *Sociological Perspectives* 59, no. 1 (2016): 27-45; Agustín, *Sex at the Margins.*

35 Weitzer, "The Mythology of Prostitution."

36 Weitzer, R. (2009b). "Sociology of sex work."*Annual Review of Sociology,* 35, 213–234

37 Weitzer, "The Mythology of Prostitution."

38 https://www.eavesforwomen.org.uk/about-eaves/our-projects/the-poppy-project/

39 https://prostitutionresearch.com/about/mission/.

40 Awaken Non-profit Organization | Human Trafficking In Nevada (awakenreno.org).

41 Vision, Mission, and Values – CAASE.

42 Jackson, "Sex Worker Rights."

43 Jackson, "Sex Worker Rights."

44 https://www.nswp.org/what-we-do.

45 https://www.redumbrellafund.org/about-us/history/.

46 Kempadoo, Kamala; Jo Doezema (1998). *Global Sex Workers.* Routledge. 9780415918299.

47 www.coyotela.org/what_is.html

48 DesireeAlliance | Civil, Labor, and Human Rights for All Sex Workers

49 DesireeAlliance

50 https://onestafoundation.org/about-us/

51 Minichiello, Victor, John Scott, and Denton Callander. "A New Public Health Context to Understand Male Sex Work." *BMC Public Health* 15, no. 1 (2015): 282–282; Makhakhe, Nosipho Faith, Anna Meyer-Weitz, Helen Struthers, and James McIntyre. "The role of health and advocacy organizations in assisting female sex workers to gain access to health care in South Africa." *BMC Health Services Research* 19, no. 1 (2019): 746–746.

52 Makhakhe et al, "The Role of Health and Advocacy Organizations"; Platt, Lucy, Pippa Grenfell, Rebecca Meiksin, Jocelyn Elmes, Susan G. Sherman, Teela Sanders, Peninah Mwangi, and Anna-Louise Crago. "Associations between sex work laws and sex workers' health: A systematic review and meta-analysis of quantitative and qualitative studies." *PLoS Medicine* 15, no. 12 (2018): e1002680.

53 Minichiello et al., "A new public health context."

54 https://law.yale.edu/ghjp/projects/gender-sexuality-and-rights/protecting-health-and-rights-sex-workers-us-and-globally.

55 https://www.stjamesinfirmary.org.

56 Vik, "I Don't Let."

57 Burleson "Emotional Support Skills."

58 Burleson "What Counts as Effective."

59 Vik, "I Don't Let."

Chapter 3

Sex Work is Real Work

Benefits and Obstacles to Personal Autonomy in the Sex Industry

Amelia Walker

Feminist scholarship about sex work has often been contentious. While many believe in the abolition of the sex industry, others are working to reduce stigma and decriminalize sex work and sex workers. It is crucial to prioritize voices of those in the sex work community to understand how to effectively support this community. Some define sex work as a wide range of activities related to prostitution, pornography, stripping, etc., while other definitions have more nuanced conceptions.[1] While many forms of sex work exist, each of them are "subject to varying degrees of stigma and are thus worthy of examination together."[2] Sex work is a topic widely considered taboo, residing at the intersection of opposing desires in our culture.[3] This is a dangerous intersection at which competing discourses about sex work meet. Stigma often results in exclusion because of secrecy and shame, leading to the marginalization of certain groups and identities, having negative implications for the well-being of these individuals.[4] Derogatory labels such as "whore" and "hooker" are disgracing markers which work to place shame and stigma on sex workers, which often show up in law, media, social policies, and research relating to sex work, resulting in sex workers facing ineffective and violent policy choices that have negative impacts on their working conditions, experiences, and overall well- being.[5] Structures of power maintain the cycle of stigma, preserving hierarchies that place female-identifying sex workers in the margins.[6] Prior research in this arena has been regarded as stigmatizing.[7] The negative framing of sex work results in the failure to produce cohesive understandings and effective responses to the needs of sex workers.

Discourses about the abolition of the sex work industry frame sex workers as victims of exploitation needing to be saved. Neoabolitionists believe sex work is inherently violent and seek to eradicate the sex trade, an approach often adopted by radical feminists.[8] Radical feminists frame sex work as inherently violent and exploitative.[9] Radical feminists conceptualize prostitution as an abuse of human rights regardless of whether it is voluntary or forced; they have had a significant impact on the creation of anti-trafficking legislation at national and international levels.[10] Others understand sex work as it "exists along a continuum of power, agency, and agreement."[11] The sex workers rights movement, for example, was founded on three ideas based in the agency of the individual: many women choose sex work freely; sex work should be regarded and respected as legitimate work; and denying a woman the opportunity to be a sex worker is a violation of a woman's civil rights.[12] Sex work should be recognized as a legitimate form of work and not just another oppressive feature of the patriarchy.[13]

Marxist feminists support ideas that sex workers, like workers in any other labor force, are subject to exploitation, bringing into discussion the political and economic contexts in which sex work occurs.[14] Most labor forces, including sex work, consist of varying degrees of coercion, exploitation, resistance, and agency, suggesting that sex work should be discussed within an understanding that sex worker experiences range in degrees of empowerment/choice to oppression/exploitation.[15] It should also be noted that the notion of empowerment often creates a false victim versus criminal narrative, and "that one should not have to feel empowered by sex work in order to engage in it."[16] Examining, recognizing, and validating the different experiences and voices of women who have worked in the industry is imperative to confront the realities of these laborers.[17] Sex work can simultaneously act as a site of subversion and agency, and exploitation and victimization.[18] Understanding that exploitation is not unique to sex work can help us resist attempts to regard power as overwhelming and all-consuming of the subject.[19] Criminalization exposes sex workers to stigma and mistreatment from the criminal justice system.[20] To understand sex work beyond a binary frame of criminalization versus decriminalization, feminists should apply intersectional analyses to sex work instead of single-issue analyses.[21]

Moral arguments, such as good versus bad dichotomies, fail to address the needs and political desires of sex workers, especially non-white sex workers.[22] The recent passage of laws such as FOSTA/SESTA (Fight Online Sex Trafficking Act and Stop Enabling Sex Traffickers Act) in the US exemplify how good versus bad narratives can generalize sex work and conflate it with sex trafficking. FOSTA and SESTA reproduce sex work stigma by framing all forms of sex work as exploitative and conflating sex work with sex trafficking.[23] It is important to acknowledge that grouping the two together results in a misunderstanding of the different needs of those who want to be involved in the industry and those who are forced into it/want to leave.[24] From 1998 to 2008, the online sector of sex work resulted in a 50 percent increase in industry size.[25] The online expansion of the sex work industry has greatly improved the working conditions of many sex workers, allowing them to work independently and trade information with other sex workers regarding safety.[26] It mitigated harm by allowing them to avoid street work or going through exploitative third-party agencies and provided more financial security and physical safety.[27] Online advertising allows sex workers the time and ability to screen clients' backgrounds to ensure safety.[28] Indoor/online sex workers experience less exposure to violence and police.[29] Peterson, Robinson, and Shih surveyed 262 sex workers in a 2019 study concerning the impact of FOSTA/SESTA.[30] A reported 92 percent of survey participants said that they screened clients before the passage of FOSTA/SESTA. However, only 63 percent reported screening clients after the laws' passage, and 70 percent reported a loss of income since the enactment of the laws.[31] FOSTA/SESTA has affected sex workers' access to screening clients for safety measures and strains their means of earning a living. Anti-trafficking laws encourage the criminalization of online sex work presence as well as the criminalization of migrant and street-based sex workers and their clients.[32]

Conflating sex work with human trafficking does little to protect victims of trafficking and further exploits sex workers by encouraging criminality, ignoring complexities, misallocating resources, increasing the risk of violence, and creating barriers to legal, medical, and social services.[33] Banks, as well as other payment services such as PayPal, are being pressured to close accounts of individuals suspected of trafficking, resulting in sex workers losing access to their accounts and their money.[34] Laws such as FOSTA/SESTA "make it illegal for social services to market material to sex workers."[35] FOSTA/SESTA policymakers stated their goal was to reduce human trafficking by holding internet platforms accountable for the content their users post.[36] This allows owners of websites to be prosecuted if they were found engaging in the facilitation or promotion of prostitution; no effort made the distinction between consensual sex work and sex trafficking.[37]

These laws have instead increased the pressure on internet platforms to censor their users, leading to an increase of exposure and violence, leaving those who rely on sex work as a primary form of income without many of the resources to which they once had access to keep themselves and each other safe.[38] The Federal Bureau of Investigstion (FBI) seized Backpage, an online platform that allowed sex workers to find and screen clients, days before the laws had passed.[39] VerifyHim, another site that sex workers used to reduce the chance of harm, was also taken down after the passing of FOSTA/SESTA.[40] Other sites such as Google and Craigslist began to remove content related to sex work, along with many other networks that sex workers use for advertising such as Twitter and Instagram.[41] Because of the loss of advertising avenues on Backpage, many sex workers were pushed to mediate their reduced income by returning to street-based sex work or brothels.[42] Social media platforms are likely to keep removing and restricting sexual content as they seek to grow and monetize their user bases.[43] Since the passage of FOSTA/SESTA, social media sites have been increasingly deleting and censoring content that can be interpreted as promoting or facilitating prostitution.[44] Some scholars suggest working toward breaking up monopolies by social media giants (such as Facebook and Google) and pressing for transparency and clarity in decisions about user data and content.[45]

Sex workers and sex work advocates such as Liara Roux have taken to the internet to address topics and concerns relating to sex workers, including sex workers' rights. In 2018, Roux used a popular online forum called Reddit to host a Q&A, bringing together sex work organizers and advocates, trafficking survivors, researchers, educators, legal experts, policymakers, politicians, sex workers, and a curious public.[46] Online discussion sites of discussion such as this one are ripe with information, experience, expertise, and thoughtful considerations of the reality and future of sex work. Discourse that emphasizes sex workers in discussions about sex work should be explored to better understand the realities and experiences of these individuals, and to create more effective solutions with those most affected included in those conversations and decisions.

RESEARCH QUESTIONS

RQ1: How can the use of critical thematic analysis (CTA) aid in the critical analysis of comments submitted to Roux's Ask Me Anything (AMA)?

RQ2: How can feminist theory help us understand themes from the data as benefits or obstacles to sex workers' personal autonomy?

METHOD

A typology was developed from comments posted under four umbrella questions submitted to Roux's 2018 Ask Me Anything, hosted via Reddit under the subreddit r/IAmA. Subreddits are topic-specific comment threads. r/IAMA is a subreddit individuals use to introduce themselves and their craft, commonly used by sex workers to gain attention to their business. Four data tables were created respective to the four questions chosen. The questions were selected through Reddit's comment filter feature which chooses the "best" comments through an algorithm which considers the "best" comments as those with the highest upvote to downvote ratio. Essentially, upvotes are considered "likes" and downvotes are considered "dislikes." Comments were analyzed for critical themes based on three criteria including recurrent, repetitive, and forceful discourse. Themes were then coded for frequency to identify the most common topics of discourse in this particular set of data, and divided into two categories including sex work benefits and sex work obstacles to personal autonomy based on comment submitters' positive or negative framing of themes. Reddit user names were omitted in the interest of privacy.

Social media can help researchers gain more knowledge of their subjects and make more informed decisions when conducting research.[47] Using US Reddit for data collection can be beneficial to researchers as it has the potential for lifting traditionally marginalized voices, valuable to researchers in its ability to inspire new framings and questions for experts through public engagement and provide new insights to experts and policymakers.[48] Data gathered from social media such as Reddit can provide new knowledge to policymakers and influence them to make more informed decisions.[49] Through public engagement, experts can provide knowledge and facts needed to make informed decisions, generate interest, and improve public support.[50] Reddit AMAs such as the one hosted by Roux can generate useful dialogue between experts and the general public.[51]

Critical thematic analysis is the methodological framework used for this study. CTA is useful in identifying the interrelationships between discourse, ideologies, practices, and power relations.[52] CTA aids critical scholars in identifying the power embedded in certain ideologies through examinations of patterns in discourse, giving attention to hierarchies that can then be critically analyzed.[53] CTA relies on three criteria including recurrence (at least two parts contain the same thread of meaning), repetition (at least two parts contain the same wording or phrasing), and forcefulness (the presence of emphasis) to identify critical themes from a set of data.[54] This study uses CTA to identify sex worker experiences in relationship to larger ideologies and social practices to better understand the influence discourse has on policy, and the influence policy has on those in the sex work industry. This method helps highlight experiences and concerns relating to sex work by exploring public discourse among sex workers, feminists, advocates, and organizers, aiding in the understanding of the needs and political desires of those in the sex work industry. Feminist theory guides critical perspectives in this research. Adopting a feminist lens aids in using the disruptive potential of resistance to power and challenges hierarchical ideologies harmful to sex workers.[55] A critical feminist lens is used to identify themes as benefits or obstacles to sex worker personal autonomy.

RESULTS

Four tables (see appendix) were created respective to the four initial questions selected from the AMA. Eleven themes were identified throughout the data sets (see appendix for themes, descriptions, and examples). Themes were categorized by the framing of topics as either beneficial to or obstacles to personal autonomy. Table 1 indicates that three posts concern stigma, two posts concern sex work as legitimate work, two posts concern criminalization, two posts concern exploitation, and one post concerns morality.[56] Table 2 indicates that two posts concern criminalization, two posts concern sex work vs. sex trafficking, two posts concern exploitation, and one post concerns consent.[57] Table 3 indicates that eleven posts concern job autonomy, eleven posts concern pleasure, five posts concern income (in)stability, four posts concern stigma, two posts concern criminalization, and one post concerns exploitation.[58] Table 4 indicates that eight posts concern criminalization, five posts concern censorship, three posts concern sex work vs. sex trafficking, two posts concern exploitation, two posts concern stigma, one post concerns marginalization, one post concerns morality, and one post concerns sex work as legitimate work.[59]

DISCUSSION

Job autonomy and pleasure were the most frequently occurring themes throughout the data, followed by criminalization, stigma, censorship, exploitation, sex work vs. sex trafficking, income (in)stability, sex work as legitimate work, marginalization, and morality, respectively. This indicates that job autonomy and pleasure were the most discussed topics, and morality was the least recurrent topic.

Job Autonomy

Job autonomy is referred to as the freedom to make one's own decisions regarding work. To answer question three, one respondent refers to job autonomy as being a perk of sex work:

> In my case, sex work has given me a lot of freedom: being able to decide my own schedule, working when and how I want to, on my own terms. I don't have to do anything I don't want to do, and all effort I put into my work directly benefits me [yay, self employment!]. It has also given me a lot of financial freedom.

The respondent notes their "freedom" to decide their work schedule and their work responsibilities, as well as the financial freedom they experience from being a self-employed sex worker. "Freedom" frames this individual's experience of sex work in terms of job autonomy. "On my own terms" indicates this individual acts as their own boss. "I don't do anything I don't want to do" exemplifies the autonomy and choice the individual is granted by running her own business. Job autonomy can be considered a means of liberation for women and other marginalized identities by allowing for personal freedom to be one's own boss and make one's own decisions. "All effort I put into my work directly benefits me" indicates that job autonomy is beneficial to this individual.

Pleasure

Pleasure is referred to as finding enjoyment in sex work. To answer question three, one respondent explains finding pleasure in their job as a sex work:

> I absolutely love my job. After years of wandering and feeling lost, I've found the profession that fits my personality and strengths more than any other. The rewards are unbelievable. I've developed deep friendships. I feel like I'm really creating a difference in peoples' lives. As an example, a severely depressed client hugged me so hard, started to cry, and told me, "Thank you for letting me feel again." It's moments like these that make me so passionate about what I do.

This individual uses "love" to define how they feel about being a sex worker. The short anecdote shows this individual has positive experiences of sex work and finds pleasure in making others feel good. "Passionate about what I do" indicates the level of enthusiasm this individual has for being a sex worker. "The rewards are unbelievable" indicate this individual has gained from their involvement in the sex work industry. Narratives of pleasure are important in conversations about sex work, as they challenge dominant notions of sex work as inherently oppressive. Sex workers can experience pleasure doing sex work just as a construction worker might find pleasure in building houses. Pleasure can also act as empowerment, an aspect of liberation with potential to disrupt harmful narratives of sex work and sex workers.

Criminalization

Criminalization refers to the laws in place which regard sex work as criminal/illegal. To answer question four, one respondent discusses the impacts of FOSTA/SESTA:

> Repealing them is an absolute necessity. FOSTA/SESTA has done the exact opposite of its intent. It continues our government's obsession with punishment over actual results. Not only that, it is an incredible infringement on free speech. One of the biggest effects of FOSTA/SESTA has not been on advertising, but on activism. The work we do is illegal and therefore, the support we provide for each other is often illegal. We cannot fight for each other if we cannot speak to each other, and this legislation has made it near impossible for us to use the largest forum of communication, the internet.

This individual regards FOSTA/SESTA as an "incredible infringement on freedom of speech," insisting that these laws are unconstitutional. They also note the effect these laws have had on sex workers' ability to provide each other support and be in conversation with each other by criminalizing their activity on the internet and limiting their access to each other. This individual also notes that these laws focus on "punishment over actual results" insisting that punishment is an ineffective approach. Criminalization further compromises the safety of those vulnerable to exploitation. Sex workers use the internet to share information, organize, and protect each other. Laws such as FOSTA/SESTA sever sex worker ties to their community and expands potential for harm.

Stigma

Stigma refers to the negative social perceptions which demean sex work and sex workers. In response to question three, one respondent describes stigma as being the worst part of their job as a sex worker:

> The worst thing about this job? The social isolation because we can't afford to live like others. For example, two days ago, a neighbor came by and invited me to join a book club that would meet once a month. I love to read, and the idea was so intriguing. However, I can't afford to get too close or I could endanger my life and the [lives] of those I help. Just not a good idea. I would be open to people trying to get to know me on the outside and from personal experience it only takes one who recognizes you and is an 'anti,' as we call them, and my wonderful life would be over. To me that is the worst . . .

This individual regards social isolation as being the worst part of their job in the sex industry, and suggests sex workers cannot exactly live the same way others do because of the stigma placed on their jobs. "It only takes one who recognizes you and is an 'anti,' as we call them" insists that living without caution could result in being outed and therefore endangering their own lives. The stigma faced by sex workers perpetuates cycles of violence and criminalization. Being outed is a common fear among sex workers who wish to remain anonymous, one that can have life-changing effects on an individual. Outing someone is a violent act because it makes an individual vulnerable to ostracization, arrest, and abuse. Sex work stigma influences policy, often resulting in the failure to address safety needs and to implement effective protection practices.

Censorship

Censorship refers to the suppression of sex workers' online freedom. To answer question four, one respondent offers their views on censorship as a result of FOSTA/SESTA:

> Any law that criminalizes speech must be repealed. It doesn't just affect the supposed target, it affects everyone's speech. The only way to criminalize forms of speech is to surveil everyone. So civilians have a vested interest in deposing these initiatives as well. I think for most civilians—who have from many angles been conditioned to ostracize sex workers—it is a challenge to understand that our interests are aligned here. They are.

This individual suggests that more civilians should vouch for the repeal of FOSTA/SESTA because laws that criminalize freedom of speech affect everyone, subjecting them to "surveillance" and infringing on privacy. The individual also suggests that most people find it difficult to understand that the interests of sex workers and civilians can be aligned because of the ostracization of sex workers. Censorship directly affects the sex work community in negative ways by restricting sex workers' access to information, resources, and social media platforms, limiting their ability to safely generate income.

Exploitation

Exploitation is referred to as taking advantage of an individual or group for profit. In response to question four, one respondent explains why they believe FOSTA/SESTA should be repealed:

> It should absolutely be repealed, and we should be lobbying for decriminalization of sex work instead. Why? Because FOSTA/SESTA, in my opinion, are not at all about trafficking. . . . FOSTA/SESTA was the government's [unfortunately successful] attempt at a federal anti-prostitution law which did not exist in the past. They intentionally conflated the two to cause a panic. . . . In reality, people get trafficked all the time—for domestic labor, farm labor, even to do your nails. And while

there are already anti-trafficking laws in place that are clearly
not being enforced, the government seized the opportunity to
create this law. Not because they care about trafficked children
and teens, but because it was a convenient way to get rid of the
pesky prostitute problem.

This individual suggests that FOSTA/SESTA are less about trafficking
and more about intentionally targeting sex workers who engage in prostitution. "The pesky prostitute problem" insists that the governments see this form
of sex work as an issue to be solved with punishment. They note that trafficking is not unique to the sex industry with their mention of the exploitation
of domestic laborers, farm laborers, and even nail technicians, demonstrating
that exploitation concerns labor of all sorts. This individual's comment draws
attention to dominant ideologies that frame sex work as a "problem" and the
presence of this ideology in sex work policy. They highlight how these ideologies lack an informed understanding of the differences between consensual
sex work and sex trafficking, and how the conflation of the two influences
public opinion.

Sex work vs. sex trafficking
Sex work vs. sex trafficking refers to the distinctions or lack thereof made
between sex work and sex trafficking. To answer question two, one respondent
offers their distinction between being a consensual sex worker and being a survivor of trafficking:

> So I am a trafficking survivor, and I am a current sex worker.
> There is a huge difference between voluntary sex work and
> having a pimp control your every action. I wasn't allowed
> to pee with one pimp! I also found clients walking on the
> streets, and [I] was forced to do what they paid ty! Nowadays,
> I do everything online and I can say no even if I was tipped
> to do something, because I'm in control of my body like it
> should be!

This individual offers their unique positionality as a sex worker who was a
trafficking survivor. "Control your every action," "forced," and "wasn't allowed"
exemplify the exploitation this individual faced while being trafficked by a
pimp, and the absence of consent. "Nowadays I do everything online . . . I'm in

control of my body like it should be" exemplifies the free will this individual now has over their engagement with sex work and the voluntary nature of their choice. "I'm in control" emphasizes sex work as a personal and consensual choice for this individual, and indicates a level of personal autonomy. This individual is uniquely positioned to provide insight as both a sex trafficking survivor and voluntary sex worker, and makes a clear distinction between the exploitation one is subjected to as a trafficked person and the free-willed nature of being a voluntary sex worker. Their personal experience challenges the notion that sex work and sex trafficking are the same, and disrupts narratives of sex work as inherently coercive.

Income (In)stability

Income (in)stability refers to the degree to which income is consistent. To answer question three, one respondent explains the inconsistent nature of their income from sex work:

> Best perk: I get to have sex and do things I enjoy in exchange for the money that I need to take care of myself as a disabled person! And the notoriety ain't bad either. Worst: It's feast or famine, and there's not as much stability as I would like. But it doesn't make my job not worth it. I love sex work! I couldn't imagine doing anything else! I always wanted to be a sex worker.

This individual suggests that the nature of sex work is "feast or famine," indicating that sometimes the money is good and sometimes it is not. "There is not as much stability as I would like" insists on the inconsistency in their income. This statement disrupts the common notion that sex work is fast and easy money. Although this individual experiences inconsistent income, they regard sex work as the best option for them. Sex work allows them to take care of themself "as a disabled person," a claim which disrupts another common notion that sex work is a desperate means for survival. This person lives with a disability and is able to generate enough income through self employment to support themself. This individual "couldn't imagine doing anything else," insisting that even though income is inconsistent, the benefits of their engagement with sex work outweigh the obstacles. This individual finds personal autonomy through being able to provide for themselves in ways they can enjoy. Money is not the driving factor for this individual's engagement in sex work, though they are still able to support themselves and find enjoyment in their work.

Sex work as legitimate work

Sex work as legitimate work refers to the recognition that sex work is paid labor and should be regarded as legitimate work. In response to question one, one respondent explains why sex work is real work:

> That sex work is work. I can't say this enough. We are in a labor industry. Period, end of story. Once the outside world gets this, then we can move forward and achieve the same rights as other citizens. Why is this so important? For those of you out there who want to stop trafficking, this is how it occurs.

This individual emphasizes that the sex industry is a labor industry. "Labor" indicates that the work in which sex workers are engaging takes a certain amount of physical, mental, and social effort to provide a service to others. The individual also notes that not recognizing sex work as real work leads to the exploitation and trafficking of workers because they are not granted "the same rights as other citizens." This suggests that recognizing sex work as a legitimate form of labor can aid in the fight against trafficking by allowing better working conditions and reducing the risk for exploitation. This recognition also has potential to challenge stigma and social attitudes toward sex work. Recognizing sex work as a legitimate form of labor is a step in the direction of restoring the rights sex workers are denied and advocating for better policy and protections.

Marginalization

Marginalization refers to the exclusion of certain groups of individuals. To answer question four, one respondent explains how FOSTA/SESTA leads to the marginalization of sex workers:

> There is no "fixing" this law. Everything this law does is harmful. It further marginalizes sex workers and increases our vulnerability to trafficking and abusive work conditions. It does this in multiple and intersecting ways.
>
> Starting over means that all legislation that impacts the lives of sex workers and trafficking survivors must be written with the input of both workers and survivors. Many in our community have had experiences with both abusive/coercive conditions and safe or safer conditions. That makes us experts, collectively,

on the difference between those situations. Any policy written without our input will, like FOSTA, completely fail.

This individual regards FOSTA/SESTA as "harmful" because the laws further marginalize sex workers by increasing their vulnerability by subjecting them to exploitation and trafficking. "Multiple and intersecting ways" emphasizes the complex, structural nature of the harm perpetuated by ineffective laws. They also note this effectiveness to be a result of the laws being written without input from either sex workers or trafficking survivors, and they suggest that policies written without the input of the subjects themselves will fail and further endanger the lives of those the laws claim to protect.

Morality

Morality refers to concepts of right and wrong which are used in arguments against sex work. To answer question one, one respondent speaks on the subject of morality as it relates to perceptions of sex work and sex workers:

> Sex work is work, and it's service industry work. Pretending that it's inherently different than other service industry work for any other reason than the fact that it's stigmatized is buying into the belief that sex is uniquely special to women and has a unique moral impact on our worth. It sounds so obvious stated like that, but people never do interrogate their belief systems this far. So right now, some guy is telling me how different and special sex is than waiting tables, all because it involves genitals. It's not different. It's not more special. My value and integrity [are] not located in my genitals any more than it is in my hands when I changed diapers.

This individual suggests that stigma often comes from a politics of morality placed onto women which claims sex to be "uniquely special to women and has a unique moral impact on our worth." Sex is used as the moral to gauge a woman's worth. This individual compares sex work to other forms of gendered labor, suggesting that "value and integrity" are not located in their genitals to any greater extent than it is in their hands when they change diapers. This puts into perspective how morality and worth are used to challenge pro-sex work narratives, but are absent from consideration in other contexts. Moral arguments are a roadblock to the liberation of sex workers. Morality has historically been used to demean and devalue women and keep them subordinate to patriarchy, and it remains a driving factor for sex work stigma.

Benefits to Personal Autonomy

Respondents' discourse about these aforementioned topics show that job autonomy, pleasure, sex work is legitimate work, and income stability can be recognized as being beneficial to sex workers' personal autonomy. Job autonomy allows women to work freely and independently without coercion, and it is noted positively throughout the data sets. Being in control of one's financial pursuits can be seen as a means of liberation in that it allows one to make work-related decisions with their best interest in mind. Job autonomy allows sex workers to avoid exploitation and the risk associated with street-based work. Respondents who mentioned pleasure note their engagement in sex work as an enjoyable and rewarding experience, a notion which challenges the narrative that sex workers are victims needing to be saved. Sex workers can and do have positive and life-enriching experiences in the sex industry. Pleasure is read as a beneficial part of sex work and is experienced in various ways, an opposition to the idea that all sex workers are victims. Respondents who mentioned sex work as legitimate work emphasize this as a necessary acknowledgment.

Recognizing sex work as real work and part of the labor industry positively contributes to perceptions of sex work validity. A common phrase used by sex workers and advocates, "Sex work is real work," demands that sex work is seen as a valid form of labor worthy of rights and protection. This narrative aids in achieving personal autonomy by opposing the stigma about sex as an invalid means of income. More recognition that sex work is legitimate work would change the discourse about sex work socially and legally, and aid in decriminalization and destigmatization of sex work. Income stability (as opposed to instability) was regarded positively. Voluntary sex work allows many sex workers more financial freedom than they might have with other jobs. Stable income from self employment allows sex workers to be autonomous by providing the means necessary for survival and economic mobility on their own terms. One respondent notes that the income they receive from sex work helps them provide for themselves as a person living with disability, highlighting the general concern over disability resources that this individual manages through consensual sex work. These aspects of sex work can be regarded as a means of liberation from practices that keep women and marginalized populations dependent on a system which fails to properly address the needs of these populations to survive and thrive independently. Job autonomy, pleasure, sex work is legitimate work, and income stability are all associated positively with personal autonomy in the sex industry, and they can be understood as beneficial to achieving personal autonomy.

Obstacles to Personal Autonomy

Income instability (as opposed to income stability), stigma, criminalization, exploitation, censorship, sex work versus sex trafficking, marginalization, and morality are interpreted as obstacles to personal autonomy. Income instability is an obstacle because the inconsistent flow of money is difficult to predict. Income instability has been worsened by laws such as FOSTA/SESTA that limit sex workers' ability to conduct business online in addition to the seizing of accounts of individuals suspected of trafficking. Income is directly linked to the material conditions of sex workers as it determines their potential to survive and thrive. Stigma is a roadblock to decriminalization and quality of life. Sex work stigma negatively affects public opinion and discourse, which leaks into laws and policy about sex workers. Stigma is an obstacle to personal autonomy because of its potential to influence perceptions, decisions, and practices with power to shape the lived conditions of sex workers. Criminalization acts as an obstacle to personal autonomy as it results in life-changing consequences for sex workers. Many sex workers agree on decriminalization as a preferred course of action.

Anti-trafficking laws such as FOSTA/SESTA further put sex workers at risk for harm by limiting their access to resources and support, restricting their means to generate income, and subjecting them to legal consequences. Decriminalization is commonly the most favored by sex workers and sex work advocates opposed to legalization as it affords certain power and rights to sex workers and is most productive in terms of creating safer conditions and sex work well-being.[60] Decriminalization is the only evidence-based policy that works to protect sex workers.[61] Exploitation, regarded negatively by respondents, is an obstacle to achieving personal autonomy and general safety. Respondents associated exploitation with trafficking rather than voluntary sex work, drawing a difference between voluntary sex work and sex trafficking. Exploitation is an obstacle to personal autonomy in that it strips the individual of personal choice and protections against mistreatment.

Censorship was regarded negatively and is an obstacle to personal autonomy. Censorship has resulted in the taking down of websites that sex workers used for safety measures and to promote business, resulting in a significant loss of income for these individuals. Censorship restricts sex worker autonomy by suppressing their means to work safely and independently. Sex work versus sex trafficking was associated negatively because the conflation between the two criminalizes the actions of voluntary sex workers, putting them at risk for trafficking while doing little to combat sex trafficking itself. Respondents expressed dismay for discourse that fuse the two together and for the ramifications that are the result of such discourse. Equating the two results in a misunderstanding of the labor conditions under which each practice operates, the misallocation of resources intended to help, and uninformed decisions about perception and policy.

Marginalization keeps sex workers from being able to access the proper resources, rights, and protections. This exclusion portrays sex workers as unimportant, perpetuating an environment which condones harm. Morality was associated negatively and acts as an obstacle to personal autonomy. Morality is often used in anti-sex work discourse and used as a justification for the stigma about exchanging sexual services for money. Morality politics support narratives that engaging in sex work decreases a woman's worth and value, inspiring negative public opinions and maintaining cycles of harm. Income instability, stigma, criminalization, exploitation, censorship, sex work versus sex trafficking, marginalization, and morality act as obstacles to personal autonomy through their potential to keep sex workers dependent on hegemonic systems shaped to impede their ability to thrive independently.

ANALYSIS

Developing a typology of comments submitted to Liara Roux's Ask Me Anything has allowed for the identification of certain topics of concern to those in the sex work industry. This typology helps us to understand the topics of discussions that sex workers are engaging in, giving us insight to potential benefits and obstacles to their personal autonomy. It is critical that discussions about policy and sex work include sex workers to prevent the spread of misinformation, combat stigma, and create effective solutions with their well-being in mind.

To answer Research Question 1, using critical thematic analysis has aided in identifying critical patterns in discourse about sex work, highlighting sex worker-produced knowledge, and advocating for their best interest by providing a critical lens which gives important attention to the specific contexts which place and keep sex workers in the margins of society. CTA aided in identifying the eleven themes in Roux's Reddit AMA: exploitation, sex work vs. trafficking, criminalization, job autonomy, pleasure, stigma, sex work is work, morality, income (in)stability, censorship, and marginalization. Recognizing these themes as critical topics of discussion allows insight into the concerns of sex workers because they have important implications for the future of sex workers. Knowledge produced by sex workers should be recognized as valid and included in decisions that have potential to shape, disrupt, or improve their lives.

To answer Research Question 2, feminist theory helps us understand the nature of sex worker inequality by identifying and uncovering the interdependence of the critical topics mentioned above in terms of benefits or obstacles to personal autonomy, exposing the power dynamics maintaining the oppression of this historically marginalized population which keep them vulnerable to harm. Recognizing this systematic inequality demands attention to how certain narratives and practices contribute to the damage done to communities that have been denied proper rights and protections.

LIMITATIONS AND FUTURE RESEARCH

These findings are not without their limitations. This study could be improved with research methods that prioritize the lived experiences and stories of participants, such as narrative and ethnography, which will provide researchers with a fruitful avenue to further explore these categories. It has been emphasized that research about sex work should include input from sex workers, which includes first-hand accounts of experiences. Narrative and ethnographic methods combined with critical analysis would allow deeper and more authentic insights into the lives and political desires of sex workers. Other limitations include the overlapping of themes identified from the data sets. While this has helped understand the structural nature and complex links among the issues discussed above, having clearer distinctions between themes could expand analyses into broader directions.

Future research should investigate the specific impact of federal and state laws on sex workers of color. Discourse from anti-sex trafficking positions often construct narratives of the innocent victim who is forced into sex work as being the only ones deserving of help.[62] Protection practices ultimately exclude and criminalize some individuals on the basis of race, leaving them absent from legal consideration.[63] This practice leaves out women and girls of color, namely Black women and girls who are often already criminalized based on their race, by assuming they engage in sex work by choice.[64] The structural oppression Black women face goes disregarded in anti-trafficking discourse.[65] Future research should give critical attention to the unique positionality of Black sex workers because their experiences of racism in the sex work industry significantly influence how they engage with social services, dynamics that must be addressed to effectively confront the failure of policies to protect those most vulnerable to exploitation.[66]

CONCLUSION

Harmful discourses about sex work influence policy and social perceptions, ultimately creating the conditions that sex workers are struggling to overcome. It is crucial we listen to the voices of those in the sex industry to understand how to effectively support them and include them in important decisions about policy and advocacy. CTA aided in the identification and analysis of eleven critical themes found in the data, pointing to important topics of concern for those in the sex industry and allowing insight into how negative framings of sex work result in the failure to produce cohesive understandings and effective responses to the needs of sex workers. Feminist theory provided a lens which allowed for an analysis of the power dynamics involved in the function of these critical themes in regard to sex work personal autonomy. Advocating for sex workers at interpersonal and community levels is a necessary step to generate improvement in the social and political atmospheres of sex work. There is a need for those with experience in the sex trade to be at the forefront of discussions about how society and the law should regard those involved in the industry.[67] As one AMA respondent suggests, "Nothing about us without us." Sex workers desire to be in conversation with those making critical decisions about their lives and jobs. Community-based approaches prioritize harm reduction, social equity, and dignity, as opposed to the harm caused by policing and surveillance.[68] This research emphasizes how imperative it is to adopt approaches to sex work that focus on harm reduction rather than crime and punishment to effectively support and empower sex workers.

Table 1

Table includes themes from answers to question 1: "What would you most like to tell us that no one asks about?" (Reddit User, 2018).

Themes (frequency)	Description	Example
Stigma (3)	Negative social perceptions which demean sex work and sex workers	Not being able to talk about one's job with peers or loved ones for fear of ostracization
Sex work is legitimate work (2)	Recognition that sex work is paid labor and should be regarded as legitimate	Understanding that sex work is a "real" job that combines labor with customer service skills
Criminalization (2)	Laws in place which regard sex work as criminal/illegal	SESTA/FOSTA laws criminalize sex work/ers by conflating it with sex trafficking
Exploitation (2)	Taking advantage of an individual for profit	A pimp coercing a woman into performing acts against her will and taking the profits as their own
Morality (1)	Arguments against sex work which are based on concepts of right and wrong	Regarding sex work as wrong or immoral on religious bases

Table 2

Table includes themes from answers to question 2: "Does voluntary sex work contribute to sex trafficking? If so, what does the industry do to mitigate or reduce trafficking?" (Reddit User, 2018).

Themes (frequency)	Description	Example
Exploitation (2)	Taking advantage of an individual for profit	A pimp coercing a woman into performing acts against her will and taking the profits as their own
Sex work vs. sex trafficking (2)	Distinctions made between sex work and sex trafficking, which are often conflated	Understanding that sex work is a labor industry just as any other in which exploitation happens, but is not defined by that exploitation
Criminalization (2)	Laws in place which regard sex work as criminal/illegal	SESTA/FOSTA laws criminalize sex work/ers by conflating it with sex trafficking

Table 3

Table includes themes from answers to question 3: "What's the best perk of your job? Worst?
     Do you genuinely enjoy sex work? How did you discover that is something you wanted to do?" (Reddit User, 2018).

Themes (frequency)	Description	Example
Job autonomy (11)	Freedom to make own decisions regarding work	Having control over how often and how much one works and the type of work that is done
Pleasure (11)	Finding enjoyment in sex work	Finding enjoyment in providing intimate services to clients
Income (in)stability (5)	The degree to which income is consistent	Making a lot of money one week, only to make half of that the next week
Stigma (4)	Negative social perceptions which demean sex work and sex workers	Not being able to talk about one's job with peers or loved ones for fear of ostracization
Criminalization (2)	Laws in place which regard sex work as criminal/illegal	SESTA/FOSTA laws criminalize sex work/ers by conflating it with sex trafficking
Exploitation (1)	Taking advantage of an individual for profit	A pimp coercing a woman into performing acts against her will and taking the profits as their own

Table 4

Table includes themes from answers to question 4: "So what's the answer to dealing with SESTA/FOSTA? Just repeal them and start over? Can they be fixed?" (Reddit User, 2018).

Themes (frequency)	Description	Example
Criminalization (8)	Laws in place which regard sex work as criminal/illegal	SESTA/FOSTA laws criminalize sex work/ers by conflating it with sex trafficking
Censorship (5)	The suppression of sex workers' online freedom	Certain websites being taken down, which limits the resources available to sex workers and their ability to generate income
Sex work vs. sex trafficking (3)	Distinctions made between sex work and sex trafficking, which are often conflated	Understanding that sex work is a labor industry just as any other in which exploitation happens, but is not defined by that exploitation
Exploitation (2)	Taking advantage of an individual or group for profit	A pimp coercing a woman into performing acts against her will and taking the profits as their own
Stigma (2)	Negative social perceptions which demean sex work and sex workers	Not being able to talk about one's job with peers or loved ones for fear of ostracization
Marginalization (1)	Regarded as unimportant; pushed to the side; exclusion	Lack of protections in place to keep sex workers safe from exploitation
Morality (1)	Arguments against sex work which are based on concepts of right and wrong	Regarding sex work as wrong or immoral on religious bases
Sex work is legitimate work (1)	Recognition that sex work is paid labor and should be regarded as legitimate	Understanding that sex work is a "real" job that combines labor with customer service skills

REFERENCES

Anderson, Mike, Adrianne Kunkel, and Michael Robert Dennis. "'Let's (Not) Talk About That':
Bridging the Past Sexual Experiences Taboo to Build Healthy Romantic Relationships." *The Journal of Sex Research* 48, no. 4 (2011): 381–391.

Are, Carolina. "How Instagram's Algorithm Is Censoring Women and Vulnerable Users but Helping Online Abusers." *Feminist Media Studies* 20, no. 5 (2020): 741–744.

Armstrong, Lynzi. "Decriminalisation of Sex Work in the Post-Truth Era? Strategic Storytelling in Neo-Abolitionist Accounts of the New Zealand Model." *Criminology & Criminal Justice* 21, no. 3 (2021): 369–386.

Benoit, Cecilia, S. Mikael Jansson, Michaela Smith, and Jackson Flagg. "Prostitution Stigma and Its Effect on the Working Conditions, Personal Lives, and Health of Sex Workers." *The Journal of Sex Research* 55, no. 4-5 (2018): 457–471.

Blunt, Danielle, and Ariel Wolf. "Erased: The Impact of FOSTA-SESTA and the Removal of Backpage on Sex Workers." *Anti-Trafficking Review*, no. 14 (2020): 117–21.

Bronstein, Carolyn. "Pornography, Trans Visibility, and the Demise of Tumblr." *Transgender Studies Quarterly* 7, no. 2 (2020): 240–254.

Brooks, Siobhan. "Innocent White Victims and Fallen Black Girls: Race, Sex Work, and the Limits of Anti-Sex Trafficking Laws." *Signs: Journal of Women in Culture and Society* 46, no. 2 (2021): 513–521.

Chen, Kaiping, and David Tomblin. "Using Data From Reddit, Public Deliberation, and Surveys to Measure Public Opinion About Autonomous Vehicles." *Public Opinion Quarterly* 85, (2021): 289-322.

Drucker, Jesse, and Tanya Nieri. "Female Online Sex Workers' Perceptions of Exit from Sex Work." *Deviant Behavior* 39, no. 1 (2018): 1–19.

Gerassi, Lara B. "How Adult Women Who Trade Sex Navigate Social Services: A Grounded Theory Study." *Feminist Criminology* 15, no. 2 (2020): 196–216.

Grittner, Alison L, and Christine A Walsh. "The Role of Social Stigma in the Lives of Female-Identified Sex Workers: A Scoping Review." *Sexuality & Culture* 24, no. 5 (2020): 1653–1682.

Hara, Noriko, Jessica Abbazio, and Kathryn Perkins. "An Emerging Form of Public Engagement with Science: Ask Me Anything (AMA) Sessions on Reddit r/science." *PLoS ONE* 14, no. 5 (2019): 1-18.

Lawless, Brandi, and Yea-Wen Chen. "Developing a Method of Critical Thematic Analysis for Qualitative Communication Inquiry." *Howard Journal of Communications* 30, no. 1 (2019): 92-106.

Liararoux. "IAmASexWorker AMA." Reddit. June 21, 2018. https://www.reddit.com/r/IAmA/comments/8stb8o/im_liara_roux_an_escort_indie_porn_maker_and_also/

Owen, William Foster. "Interpretive Themes in Relational Communication." *Quarterly Journal of Speech* 70, no. 3 (1984): 274-287.

Peterson, Meghan, Bella Robinson, and Elena Shih. "The New Virtual Crackdown on Sex Workers' Rights: Perspectives from the United States." *Anti-Trafficking Review*, no. 12 (2019): 189–193.

Petillo, April. "Marking Embodied Borders: Compulsory Settler Sexuality, Indigeneity, and US

Law." *Women's Studies in Communication* 41, no. 4 (2018): 329–334.

Renegade, Riley, and Kressent Pottenger. "Sex Work Is Work." *New Labor Forum* 28, no. 1 (2019): 98–102.

Scoular, Jane. "The 'Subject' of Prostitution: Interpreting the Discursive, Symbolic and Material Position of Sex/Work in Feminist Theory." *Feminist Theory* 5, no. 3 (2004): 343–355.

Sloan, Lacey, and Stephanie Wahab. "Feminist Voices on Sex Work: Implications for Social Work." *Affilia* 15, no. 4 (2000): 457–479.

Sutherland, Kate. "Work, Sex, and Sex-Work: Competing Feminist Discourses on the International Sex Trade." *Osgoode Hall Law Journal* 42, no. 1 (2004): 139–168.

Tichenor, Erin. "'I've Never Been So Exploited': The Consequences of FOSTA-SESTA in Aotearoa New Zealand 1." *Anti-Trafficking Review*, no. 14 (2020): 99–115.

Valentina, Mia. "The Failures of SESTA/FOSTA." *Transgender Studies Quarterly* 7, no. 2 (2020): 237–239.

Wolf, Ariel. "Stigma in the Sex Trades." *Sexual and Relationship Therapy* 34, no. 3 (2019): 290–308.

NOTES

1   Cecilia Benoit, S. Mikael Jansson, Michaela Smith, and Jackson Flagg, "Prostitution Stigma and Its Effect on the Working Conditions, Personal Lives, and Health of Sex Workers," *The Journal of Sex Research* 55, no. 4-5 (2018), 458.

2   Benoit et al., "Prostitution Stigma," 458.

3   Mike Anderson, Adrianne Kunkel, and Michael Robert Dennis, "'Let's (Not) Talk About That': Bridging the Past Sexual Experiences Taboo to Build Healthy Romantic Relationships," *The Journal of Sex Research* 48, no. 4 (2011), 381.

4   Benoit et al., "Prostitution Stigma," 458.

5   Benoit et al, "Prostitution Stigma," 460.

6   Alison L. Grittner and Christine A Walsh, "The Role of Social Stigma in the Lives of Female-Identified Sex Workers: A Scoping Review," *Sexuality & Culture* 24, no. 5 (2020), 1671.

7   Grittner and Walsh, "The Role of Social Stigma," 1673.

8   Lynzi Armstrong, "Decriminalisation of Sex Work in the Post-Truth Era? Strategic Storytelling in Neo-Abolitionist Accounts of the New Zealand Model," *Criminology & Criminal Justice* 21, no. 3 (2021), 371.

9   Kate Sutherland, "Work, Sex, and Sex-Work: Competing Feminist Discourses on the International Sex Trade," Osgoode Hall Law Journal (1960) 42, no. 1 (2004), 151.

10   Sutherland, "Work, Sex, and Sex-Work," 141.

11   Grittner and Walsh, "The Role of Social Stigma," 1654.

12   Lacey Sloan and Stephanie Wahab, "Feminist Voices on Sex Work: Implications for Social Work," *Affilia* 15, no. 4 (2000), 467.

13   Riley Renegade and Kressent Pottenger, "Sex Work Is Work," *New Labor Forum* 28, no. 1 (2019), 102.

14   Sloan and Wahab, "Feminist Voices on Sex Work," 462.

15   Benoit et al, "Prostitution Stigma," 458.

16   Ariel Wolf, "Stigma in the Sex Trades," *Sexual and Relationship Therapy* 34, no. 3 (2019), 296.

17 Sloan and Wahab, "Feminist Voices on Sex Work," 475.

18 Sutherland, "Work, Sex, and Sex-Work," 144.

19 Jane Scoular, "The 'Subject' of Prostitution: Interpreting the Discursive, Symbolic and Material Position of Sex/work in Feminist Theory," *Feminist Theory* 5, no. 3 (2004), 352.

20 Grittner and Walsh, "The Role of Social Stigma," 1673.

21 Siobhan Brooks, "Innocent White Victims and Fallen Black Girls: Race, Sex Work, and the Limits of Anti–Sex Trafficking Laws," *Signs: Journal of Women in Culture and Society* 46, no. 2 (2021), 519-520.

22 Brooks, "Innocent White Victims and Fallen Black Girls," 514.

23 Grittner and Walsh, "The Role of Social Stigma," 1677.

24 Brooks, "Innocent White Victims and Fallen Black Girls," 514.

25 Jesse Drucker and Tanya Nieri, "Female Online Sex Workers' Perceptions of Exit from Sex Work," *Deviant Behavior* 39, no. 1 (2018), 1.

26 Erin Tichenor, "'I've Never Been So Exploited': The Consequences of FOSTA-SESTA in Aotearoa New Zealand 1," *Anti-Trafficking Review*, no. 14 (2020), 101.

27 Danielle Blunt and Ariel Wolf, "Erased: The Impact of FOSTA-SESTA and the Removal of Backpage on Sex Workers," *Anti-Trafficking Review*, no. 14 (2020), 118.

28 Meghan Peterson, Bella Robinson, and Elena Shih, "The New Virtual Crackdown on Sex Workers' Rights: Perspectives from the United States," *Anti-Trafficking Review*, no. 12 (2019), 189-190.

29 Drucker and Nieri, "Female Online Sex Workers' Perceptions of Exit from Sex Work," 2.

30 Peterson, Robinson, and Shih, "The New Virtual Crackdown on Sex Workers' Rights," 190.

31 Peterson, Robinson, and Shih, "The New Virtual Crackdown on Sex Workers' Rights," 190.

32 Tichenor, "'I've Never Been So Exploited'," 101.

33 Wolf, "Stigma in the Sex Trades," 305.

34 Mia Valentina, "The Failures of SESTA/FOSTA," *Transgender Studies Quarterly* 7, no. 2 (2020), 239.

35 Brooks, "Innocent White Victims and Fallen Black Girls," 519.

36 Blunt and Wolf, "Erased," 117.

37 Peterson, Robinson, and Shih, "The New Virtual Crackdown on Sex Workers' Rights," 189.

38 Blunt and Wolf, "Erased," 117.

39 Blunt and Wolf, "Erased," 117.

40 Blunt and Wolf, "Erased," 119.

41 Peterson, Robinson, and Shih, "The New Virtual Crackdown on Sex Workers' Rights," 189.

42 Tichenor, "'I've Never Been So Exploited'," 102.

43 Carolyn Bronstein, "Pornography, Trans Visibility, and the Demise of Tumblr," *Transgender Studies Quarterly* 7, no. 2 (2020), 250.

44 Carolina Are, "How Instagram's Algorithm Is Censoring Women and Vulnerable Users but Helping Online Abusers," *Feminist Media Studies* 20, no. 5 (2020), 742.

45 Are, "How Instagram's Algorithm Is Censoring Women," 744.

46 Liararoux, "IAmASexWorker AMA." Reddit.

47 Kaiping Chen and David Tomblin, "Using Data from Reddit, Public Deliberation, and

Surveys to Measure Public Opinion About Autonomous Vehicles," *Public Opinion Quarterly* 85, (2021), 317.

48 Chen and Tomblin, "Using Data from Reddit," 317-318.

49 Chen and Tomblin, "Using Data from Reddit," 318.

50 Noriko Hara, Jessica Abbazio, Kathryn Perkins, "An Emerging Form of Public Engagement with Science: Ask Me Anything (AMA) Sessions on Reddit r/science," *PLoS ONE* 14, no. 5 (2019), 1.

51 Hara, Abbazio, and Perkins "An Emerging Form of Public Engagement with Science," 15.

52 Brandi Lawless and Yea-Wen Chen, "Developing a Method of Critical Thematic Analysis for Qualitative Communication Inquiry," *Howard Journal of Communications* 30, no. 1 (2019), 92.

53 Lawless and Chen, "Developing a Method of Critical Thematic Analysis," 94.

54 William Foster Owen, "Interpretive Themes in Relational Communication," *Quarterly Journal of Speech* 70, no. 3 (1984), 275.

55 Scoular, "The 'Subject' of Prostitution," 352.

56 See appendix for Table 1.

57 See appendix for Table 2.

58 See appendix for Table 3.

59 See appendix for Table 4.

60 Armstrong, "Decriminalisation of Sex Work in the Post-Truth Era?," 370.

61 Peterson, Robinson, and Shih, "The New Virtual Crackdown on Sex Workers' Rights," 192.

62 Brooks, "Innocent White Victims and Fallen Black Girls," 516.

63 April Petillo, "Marking Embodied Borders: Compulsory Settler Sexuality, Indigeneity, and US Law," *Women's Studies in Communication* 41, no. 4 (2018), 333.

64 Brooks, "Innocent White Victims and Fallen Black Girls," 516.

65 Brooks, "Innocent White Victims and Fallen Black Girls," 516.

66 Lara B. Gerassi, "How Adult Women Who Trade Sex Navigate Social Services: A Grounded Theory Study," *Feminist Criminology* 15, no. 2 (2020), 211.

67 Wolf, "Stigma in the Sex Trades," 291.

68 Tichenor, "'I've Never Been So Exploited'," 115.

Chapter 4

Prostitution in the Basque Country (Euskal Herria)

Xabier Irujo

An analysis of prostitution in the Southern Basque Country should be placed within Europe's sociocultural, political, and legal paradigm. Since the end of the twentieth century, the practice of prostitution has been changing. The country of origin of the women, the types of sexual consumption, and the places that prostitution is practiced have diversified. The commercial activity itself has also changed. Today, the number of people engaging in phone sex has greatly increased, and there has been a substantial increase in the number of visits to sex websites on the internet. At the same time, poverty, armed conflicts, and other political, social, and economic problems have accelerated migration, benefiting human trafficking networks. It also places people who practice prostitution (95 percent of whom are women) in vulnerable situations because of their illegal status and limited access to communication channels and public services.[1]

In short, as pointed out in the 2003 study, "El oficio de la prostitución en Navarra: estigmas y modo de vida (The profession of prostitution in Navarra: stigmas and way of life)," there are several defining characteristics of prostitution in Europe in general and in the Basque Country in particular that can be identified in the new millennium. On the one hand, there has been a dramatic decrease in the number of native women who practice prostitution for their livelihood and a parallel increase in women from impoverished countries, most of whom lack residency or work permits. This fact has increased the state of vulnerability, labor exploitation, and social confinement of these women. On the other hand, prostitution has become a highly profitable business in the underground economy. "It has given rise to the economic enrichment of mafias and organized crime groups and the increased sexual exploitation of women working in rental apartments as well as brothels (known as clubes de alterne, or socializing clubs). The management of these apartments and brothels is governed by the plaza (or turf) system."[2] There has also been an increase in the number of transgender men and women who practice prostitution, representing 5 percent of the total number of sex workers at the start of the twenty-first century. Finally, the lack of legal and administrative measures in this area has kept the people exploited by prostitution beyond the protection of society and the law.

In 2008, about 1,820 people—the vast majority of whom were women—worked as prostitutes in the Basque Autonomous Community (BAC). This represented an increase of 2 percent since the beginning of the millennium. In the Autonomous Community of Navarra, from 500 to 775 women practiced prostitution, representing one prostituted woman for every 700 inhabitants. This rate is below the average for the Spanish state, where in 2012, 120,000 women were in prostitution or one prostituted woman for every 393 inhabitants (approximately one for every 150 adult men[3]). It was calculated that four out of every ten men had paid money in exchange for sexual practices on at least one occasion.[4] According to published data, one million men daily used the services of prostituted women at the beginning of the twenty-first century.[5]

Unlike the period before the 1990s, almost 97 percent of prostituted women practiced prostitution in apartments and brothels, while 3 percent of women offered their services on the street.[6] According to a study by Emakunde (the Basque Women's Institute), street prostitution fell by 68 percent compared to 2002, dropping from 160 women to 51. Almost half of them worked in Bizkaia (a territory with almost 50 percent of the population of the BAC) and were concentrated in three Basque municipalities, Bilbao and Galdakao in Bizkaia and Gasteiz in Araba. As Izaskun Moyua, director of Emakunde, stated, women "seek protection in a group and end up organizing among themselves to the point where the concept of the 'madame' begins to disappear."[7] This fact is cause for social alarm since these women need a certain degree of protection. The majority now have pimps (men) controlling their activity, which results in their increased exploitation. In 2008, there were 210 dwellings in the BAC where approximately 570 women worked as prostitutes, 41 percent more than in 2002. In Navarra, 430-670 of the prostituted women worked in brothels (approximately 85 percent); 40-80 women (about 10 percent) worked in apartments, and no more than 30 women (about 5 percent of the total) engaged in street prostitution.[8]

In conclusion, 66 percent of prostitution took place in brothels. However, traditional smaller brothels, averaging about four women per establishment, were replaced by "macro brothels" on the outskirts of cities, which house up to forty women. The average in the Basque Country was sixteen prostituted women per establishment.[9]

The brothels were and still are, owned by a small number of people (men in all cases) who operate monopolies. Among these men, informal agreements generate a series of "self-regulatory" rules. This explains why 50 percent of these locations take advantage of an "exchange of women" who spend twenty-one days in each establishment, correlating with their menstrual cycles.[10] This is called the "placement system."

About 90 percent of the people who practiced prostitution in the Basque Country were foreigners. They were divided into three groups: "eighteen-year-old sub-Saharan women who work on the streets; Latin American women, mostly Brazilian, from the ages of eighteen to thirty-five, who work in apartments and brothels; and young people from Eastern Europe, mostly from Romania, who rotate around different locations and homes under the close surveillance of pimps."[11] Half of the women in prostitution had children, although supporting a family was not easy considering their income. Depending on the workplace, a prostituted person could charge from €60 to €120 per service. On the street, the prices dropped to €20. In brothels, the usual rate was €60 for half an hour; the prostituted woman received 75 percent of the total wages, with the location owners keeping the rest. In other establishments, women charged a minimum of €40 and €60 per night, regardless of the services provided, and the revenue from the drinks was divided equally between them and the brothel owners.[12]

The situation has not changed much in a decade. According to data from the 2019 Emakunde report for the International Day Against Trafficking in Persons, about 2,000 women currently work as prostitutes in the Basque Country.[13] This data concurs with the report "La trata de mujeres y niñas con fines de explotación sexual en Euskadi: necesidades y propuestas (Trafficking in women and girls for the purpose of sexual exploitation in the Basque Country: needs and proposals)," prepared by a research team made up of members from the University of Deusto and the Comillas Pontifical University. According to the report, 1,968 women practiced prostitution in the Basque Country in 2018. Of these, 896 did so in brothels, 307 through agencies and "relaxation places," and 77 on the streets. There were 688 women (34.9 percent) who practiced prostitution independently by advertising on the internet, and it is estimated that 95 percent of prostituted women advertise online. The clients were mostly unpartnered men older than forty-five years of age. They generally meet in nightclubs (78 percent) or apartments (54 percent) with an average expenditure of €43-€120 per session.

The number of women who practiced prostitution for every 10,000 inhabitants at the turn of the century was 12.1 in Araba, 7.8 in Bizkaia, and 7.9 in Gipuzkoa.[14] This index is below average for the Spanish state, where in 2012, there were about 25 women practicing prostitution for every 10,000 inhabitants. The Mediterranean tourist routes, which run along the Catalan and Andalusian coasts, are known as the "Mediterranean prostitution corridor." They attract a greater number of users. A survey carried out among 500 men residing in the Basque Country shows that 19.1 percent had paid for sexual services at some point in their lives, and 3.1 percent had paid for the services of a prostitute in the last year. According to a 2008 Center for Sociological Research (CIS) survey, 32.1 percent of men in Spain had paid for sex; 10.2 percent indicated that they had only paid once, and the remaining 21.9 percent acknowledged using the services of a prostitute more than once.[15] A professor of sociology at the University of València, Antonio Ariño, authored the report "La prostitución en la Comunidad Valenciana (Prostitution in the Valencian Community)." He states that 4-6 percent are "regular customers," and 98 percent of the women interviewed stated that they had not used the services of a prostitute. When broken down by age, the data shows that men older than sixty-five pay most often to have sex: up to 40 percent.[16]

The study, titled " La trata de mujeres y niñas con fines de explotación sexual en Euskadi (Trafficking in women and girls for sexual exploitation in the Basque Country)," prepared by professor Carmen Meneses, highlights that "Bilbao was a transit area to French-speaking countries" in the sex trafficking network, leading to the rise in prostitution in the Basque Country. With the closure of borders and businesses because of COVID-19, many brothels were forced to close. Currently, as the borders reopen, the networks are being restructured.

As in the early 2000s, there were still more brothels in Bizkaia than in Araba, Gipuzkoa, and Navarra.[17] In 2017, 700-800 women were engaged in prostitution in the Autonomous Community of Navarra. That number decreased somewhat in 2021, but there is currently no reliable data. However, there is at present much more mobility, occasional relocation, and online prostitution than ever before.[18] This represents a minimum of 2,000-2,500 daily services in Navarra. The numbers rise significantly during the weeklong Festival of San Fermin when twenty to thirty services/day can be recorded per prostitute. The same high numbers can be seen after football matches in three locations near the Sadar football stadium in Iruñea-Pamplona—the Bar Miami, the Celeste Club, and Pub Rosalex. Bachelor parties also cause occasional peaks of up to 20,000 services/day.

According to the available data, there were thirty brothels in Navarra in 2008 and nineteen brothels in 2017. These numbers were reduced to ten brothels in 2021. In the last ten years, there has been an increase in prostitution taking place in apartments. As of 2017, prostitution is practiced mainly in apartments since they are more difficult for the police and court system to monitor the practice. This fact increases the invisibility and vulnerability of prostituted women.[19] In 2021, street prostitution had practically disappeared and was exercised mainly by women of Nigerian and Romanian origin in industrial parks or estates.

Generally, the apartments used are leased for up to €5,000 per month. This is well above the average rent of about €700 per month for the given area, providing insight into the enormous income generated by this underground business.[20] It is calculated that the total revenue from prostitution in the Basque Country exceeded 38.5 million euros per year in 2002.[21] Most of this money remains in the hands of "intermediaries," the real estate agencies that rent the apartments, or the pimps. It does not go to the prostituted women themselves.

Although no studies currently quantify the exact volume of the prostitution business in Navarra, estimates suggest it is enormous. Estimates for 2003 indicated that the profits obtained by a pimp running a brothel were much higher than those obtained through street prostitution, which explains the disappearance of street prostitution. In 2003, the pimps received €48 per day for room and board for each of their "tenants," along with a percentage for each service performed by the women, which used to be 20 percent (from €10 to €12). In addition, the exchange and "rental" of women between owners of brothels and plaza flats were "transactions" that go undeclared to the treasury. Twenty years ago, the average rent per "exchanged woman" was about €1,800. According to various estimates, a brothel owner pocketed €18,000-€24,000 per year for each woman, an average of six million euros annually.[22]

It has been very difficult to accurately calculate the economic profits of the prostitution business. However, since 2014, the National Statistics Institute of Spain (INE) has included an estimate of the volume of illegal activities in the annual calculation of Spain's GDP. If illegal activities account for 0.87 percent of the GDP, prostitution represents 0.35 percent, and drug trafficking represents 0.50 percent. The 2021 GDP amounted to 1,202,994 million euros; 0.35 percent of this amount represents 4,210 million euros annually.[23]

Although there is no data for Iparralde, estimates indicate that there are about 3,000 prostituted women in the entire Basque Country, and the women who practice prostitution in the Basque Country are getting younger and younger. The typical profile is a woman between the ages of eighteen and thirty-five years old, single, and with dependent children.[24] Because 80-90 percent of the prostituted women in the BAC are foreigners, they have faced an even greater vulnerability in recent years.[25] They come from economically disadvantaged countries, following the flow of migrants to Europe from South America, Asia, Africa, and Eastern Europe.[26] The data for Navarra is similar; the vast majority of women in prostitution come from Nigeria, Paraguay, Romania, Brazil, China, and the Dominican Republic. The Navarro Institute for Equality coordinates comprehensive action measures against violence against women. According to its 2017 Annual Report, four out of five of the services (80 percent) that they provided for the year were in aid of Nigerian women.[27]

As in the rest of Europe, prostitution in the Basque Country is closely linked to immigration. The increase in poverty in the countries listed above has greatly fueled the trafficking of women who come to Europe to work as prostitutes in rooms or apartments. These women have no professional alternatives and do not possess the work permits required to access the legal labor market. Many are "women between 26 and 35 years old who have unexpectedly lost their livelihoods and cannot find viable alternatives. And women over 35 years of age who were dedicated to their families, dependent on others, and whose life options changed due to a divorce, separation, widowhood, or other events."[28] They lack knowledge of the environment and the language. They also lack proper citizenship status. The isolation created by the constant rotation between brothels and the social stigma they carry prevent them from accessing social benefits or employment alternatives. Experts agree that "social isolation and exposure to health risk factors will increase the longer a person spends in prostitution. These risk factors include violence, sexually transmitted diseases, and drug addictions."[29]

Human trafficking involves coercion and threats to the relatives of the prostituted women in their native countries. According to a report by Ararteko on "La trata de personas con fines de explotación sexual en el País Vasco (Trafficking in persons for the purpose of sexual exploitation in the Basque Country)," it is common for victims to be invisible and undocumented. They possess false documentation, do not own cell phones, and are isolated "or always accompanied and controlled, suffering all kinds of rights violations: They face aggression and physical abuse if they refuse to engage in prostitution, and they also suffer psychological abuse. They are often forced to take drugs and perform humiliating and demeaning services."[30]

Adding to their socioeconomic and legal difficulties, illegal immigrants have acquired a debt that is almost impossible to repay. The debt per female prostitute of foreign origin ranges from €1,200 to €12,000, and the interest on the loan varies from 8 percent to 20 percent. Furthermore, these amounts are frequently increased by penalties of €30 to €150 each, imposed by their pimps for arbitrary reasons, such as getting up late, making the bed wrong, and talking on the phone during work hours, among other infractions.[31]

Although they can apply for a health card, these women often cannot access basic social and health assistance since they do not have a legitimate legal situation. During the pandemic, nearly the entire population of Spain was vaccinated. However, because of the high mobility of prostituted women, health centers had problems certifying and monitoring cases. In many cases, granting them a COVID-19 passport was very difficult. Regular clients "are concerned about their vaccination status, but not about using a condom." After the closure of brothels and apartments because of COVID restrictions, some of them "were welcomed" by their own clients, who did not hesitate to take a cut of their pay and "take even more advantage of the situation."[32]

The prostituted women suffer all kinds of violations,[33] but most of the attacks suffered in the practice of prostitution are not reported. The Askabide Association collects the stories and life experiences of prostituted women in an effort to explain and publicize the multiple factors that contribute to the perpetuating violence. Among the problems these women face is a "feeling that the damages they suffer are never repaired. These include psychological damages, lack of protection, the risk of future attacks, distrust in the system, experiences of revictimization and misinformation, misunderstanding, and defenselessness in court proceedings. The perception that these women lack credibility because they are prostitutes only makes the situation worse."[34]

As Satoko Kojima from the nongovernmental organization Action Against Trafficking pointed out, "between 2006 and 2016, Doctors of the World (Navarra), an international human rights organization, treated a total of 2,715 people involved in prostitution. According to the Annual Report on Monitoring and Evaluation of Compliance with the Interinstitutional Agreement for Coordination in the Face of Violence against Women in Navarra, fifty-two female victims of trafficking were assisted in 2017. More than half of these services were for women between the ages of thirty and thirty-nine, while a third corresponded to young women between the ages of eighteen and twenty-nine. The percentage of women served who did not have documentation was 31.08 percent."[35] The Mafia often attracts women through their personal profiles on social networks such as OnlyFans and TikTok.[36] Unfortunately, online marketing makes it difficult for nonprofit and governmental agencies to track the victims of trafficking to offer assistance.[37]

Sexual exploitation accounts for 50 percent of all types of trafficking. In other words, "half of the victims of trafficking in the world are sexually exploited compared to 38 percent who are trafficked for labor."[38] However, if we focus on the trafficking of women, sexual exploitation accounts for 77 percent of cases, according to the 2020 Trafficking in Persons Report of the United Nations Office on Drugs and Crime. The vast majority of victims of sexual exploitation are women (67 percent) or girls younger than 18 (25 percent). Men represent 5 percent of all cases, and boys younger than 18 represent 3 percent.

In 1935, the government of the Basque Country proclaimed a decree to abolish the regulation of prostitution. Spain joined the United Nations in 1955. During the Franco dictatorship (1936-1975), the Spanish government followed some of the regulations approved by the United Nations. For example, in 1949, the United Nations passed the Convention for the Suppression of the Traffic in Persons and the Exploitation of the Prostitution of Others. The protocol sought to help the victims of the prostitution system and promote the persecution and punishment of those persons or networks that organize the sexual exploitation of people.

The agreement made it possible for victims of prostitution to file judicial remedies against exploiters and called for international collaboration to exchange information in trafficking investigations. One of the most important points of the agreement was the adoption of measures to protect immigrants, prevent their sexual exploitation, and rehabilitate the victims. The Spanish Decree-law of March 3, 1956, on the abolition of tolerance centers and other measures related to prostitution, was abolished. In 1962, the dictatorship adhered to the United Nations Convention of 1949.[39]

In 1983, after the fall of the Franco dictatorship, the Spanish state ratified the 1979 United Nations Convention on the Elimination of All Forms of Discrimination against Women. The Beijing Declaration and Platform for Action was adopted unanimously by 189 countries during the Fourth World Conference on Women in 1995. It established that "violence against women is an obstacle to achieving the goals of equality, development, and peace, and violates and impairs the enjoyment of human rights and fundamental freedoms . . ." It also established a strategic objective "to eliminate trafficking in women and provide assistance to victims of violence derived from prostitution and sex trafficking."

In 1995, the Spanish government reformed the Penal Code.[40] The new code no longer punished those who practiced prostitution unless it involved minors or people with disabilities. It imposed sentences of five to eight years in prison for sex trafficking. Under article 177 bis of the code, trafficking is understood as "transit using violence, intimidation or deception, or abusing a situation of superiority or need or vulnerability of a national or foreign victim. Transit also included the delivery or reception of payments or benefits to the person who has control over the victim. 'Having control' was defined as being the person who captures, transports, transfers, harbors, or receives, including the exchange or transfer of control over those persons." Thus, the law prohibited the imposition of forced labor or services, slavery or practices similar to slavery, servitude or begging, sexual exploitation, including pornography, and the celebration of forced marriages."

Article 187 states that trafficking shall be understood as a person "using violence, intimidation or deceit, or abusing a situation of superiority or need or vulnerability of the victim, determines a person of legal age to exercise or stay in prostitution." Prison sentences of two to four years and a daily fine for twelve to twenty-four months would be imposed on anyone who profits from exploiting the prostitution of another person, even with their consent.[41]

The protocol to prevent, suppress, and punish trafficking in persons, especially women and children, which complements the United Nations Convention against Transnational Organized Crime, became the first legally binding international treaty in the fight against Mafias. It included a definition of human trafficking accepted in international law. It was signed in Palermo on December 15, 2000, in the presence of the secretary-general of the United Nations, Kofi

Annan, and the Italian president, Carlo Azeglio Ciampi, and was ratified by the Spanish state in December 2003.[42] One of the two protocols regulates human trafficking and the trafficking of minors. Trafficking in persons was defined in the third article as "the recruitment, transportation, transfer, harboring or reception of persons, resorting to the threat or use of force or other forms of coercion, kidnapping, fraud, deception, to the abuse of power or of a position of vulnerability or to the giving or receiving of payments or benefits to obtain the consent of a person having control over another, for the purpose of exploitation."[43] The protocol also established three areas of action in this field:

- Prevent and combat human trafficking, paying special attention to women and children.
- Protect and help the victims of such trafficking, fully respecting their human rights.
- Promote cooperation among the states to achieve these ends.

The economic development of the 1980s saw a dramatic increase in the number of foreign women in prostitution. The Organic Law 4/2000, of January 11, on the rights and freedoms of foreigners in Spain and their social integration and its reform of December 22, 2000, sought to regulate immigration to prevent the exploitation of immigrants, including sexual exploitation.[44] This law was a follow-up to the provisions of the International Convention against trafficking in persons and the exploitation of the prostitution of others ratified in 1949. Article 59 bis regulates the protection of victims of human trafficking. The law also introduced measures to broaden the fight against human trafficking and exploitation. Article 12 of Title 1, first chapter, establishes that foreigners registered in the municipality where they reside have the same right to health care as the citizens. As a result, many prostituted women can now obtain health cards and benefit from public health services.

Under Article 25 (Title 2, Chapter 1) on requirements for entry into the territory of the state, the law establishes that a foreigner who intends to enter must present the relevant legal documents, but, since prostitution is not legally regulated, these women cannot justify their employment status and obtain work permits.[45] This explains why these women enter as tourists, requesting a "stay" no longer than ninety days. After that time, they must apply for an extension or a temporary residence permit. These permits are rarely obtained, leading to these women's illegal residence status.

At the European level, the Council of Europe approved the 2011 Istanbul Convention on preventing and combating violence against women and domestic violence. This convention followed the approval of the International Convention against Trafficking in Human Beings signed in Warsaw in 2005, which prevented and combatted human trafficking, guaranteeing equality between women and men, protecting the rights of victims of trafficking, and promoting international cooperation in the field of combating human trafficking. The 2011 Istanbul Convention is the first legally binding agreement at the European level that addresses violence against women. On April 5, 2011, Directive 2011/36/EU of the European Parliament and the Council of Europe on the prevention and fight against trafficking in human beings and the protection of victims constituted an attempt to coordinate the sanctions that must be imposed in cases of human trafficking in the different member states. It also proposed the support and protective measures that should be approved to attend to victims of trafficking.

Along these same lines, the European Commission presented the report New Strategy on Combatting Trafficking in Human Beings (2021-2025) in April 2021. It "focused on crime prevention, the prosecution of traffickers, and the protection and empowerment of the victims. From 2017 to 2018, more than 14,000 victims were registered in the European Union. On a global scale, traffickers make an estimated profit of €29.4 billion in a single year."[46] Like the previous measures, the commission aims to detect, protect and assist victims of human trafficking, increase resources for the prevention of human trafficking, prosecute traffickers more actively, and improve coordination and cooperation between the main stakeholders. It also aims to better understand and respond to new trends related to all forms of human trafficking. The latest effort in this regard is the European Parliament Resolution of February 26, 2014, on sexual exploitation and prostitution and its impact on gender equality.

In line with this European legislation, the Spanish state approved the Second Comprehensive Plan to Combat Trafficking in Women and Girls for Sexual Exploitation of the Spanish State (2015-2018) to make a greater effort to:

- Prevent and detect trafficking.
- Identify, protect, and assist victims of trafficking in human beings.
- Deepen understanding of the problem in order to provide more effective responses to sexual exploitation.
- Prosecute trafficking networks more actively.
- Promote coordination and cooperation between institutions and the participation of civil society in this effort.[47]

Within this dense network of international, European, and state conventions, the Basque government included a section on prostitution in the Public Entertainment and Recreational Activities Bill in 2018. The decree draft defined the locations where prostitution took place as "establishments in whose premises sexual entertainment activities are provided or carried out freely and independently."[48] Said premises had to provide dressing rooms and rest areas for those working there. They could not be used as housing but as "public establishments where sexual leisure activities are provided or carried out freely and independently."[49] However, the government ruled out including prostitution in its catalog of public establishments and recreational activities. These are currently limited to regulating those public establishments of an erotic nature or those "aimed at entertainment for erotic or sexual purposes intended for adults."[50]

In 2021, the Basque government and the councils of Araba, Bizkaia, and Gipuzkoa decided to bolster the coordination of public and private entities to combat trafficking in women and girls. They used the framework coordinated by Emakunde, the *Instituto Vasco de la Mujer*. The director of Emakunde, Izaskun Landaida, said that a specific action protocol was created to coordinate efforts and avoid human rights violations in the Basque Country and to better identify the women trafficked for sexual exploitation.[51]

However, the firmest steps in the fight against human trafficking have taken place in Navarra. In December 2010, the Second Interinstitutional Agreement was signed for the effective coordination in the care and prevention of violence against women. They hoped to achieve "the maximum and best coordination between the institutions involved in preventing violence against women as well as delivering assistance to the victims. They established uniform guidelines for action throughout the Autonomous Community of Navarra guaranteeing quality care in health, police, judicial, and social sectors, as well as preventive work through educational and awareness-raising measures."[52]

This and other efforts made possible the approval of Provincial Law 14/2015, of April 10, to act against violence against women.[53] The Navarrese law constitutes an effort to promote research, prevention, and awareness, the detection and care of violence against women, care and recovery resources and services, the promotion of job placement, and economic autonomy. It addresses access to housing, police attention, effective protection, legal assistance, access to justice, and the right to reparation. Article 3e of the law, on the definition and manifestations of violence against women, states that "prostitution and/or sexual exploitation" means "the practice of having sexual relations with other people in exchange for money. It includes obtaining financial or other benefits from the prostitution of others (including pornographic acts or the production of pornographic material), even with their consent." The law describes prostitution as a type of "sexist violence," and is similar to legislation passed in the autonomous communities of the Canary Islands and Cantabria. It goes a step further by introducing the fundamental concept of "consent." Doctors of the World technician Maite García emphasizes that the alleged consent given by the victim to be exploited is not actual consent. It is compliance, resulting from coercion or learned helplessness. Consent cannot exist if there is a position of power, that of the person paying for services, and a position of subordination, that of the prostituted woman.

One year later, on December 2, 2016, the government of Navarra mandated the Protocol for Coordination and Action with Women and Girl Victims of Trafficking for the Purpose of Sexual Exploitation. The purpose of this protocol was to establish action guidelines for the detection, identification, care, and protection of women and girls who are victims of trafficking for sexual exploitation. It favored the coordination of the institutions involved in these processes. It also defined the relationships among the administrations responsible for addressing these matters. It identified the communication and cooperation processes among organizations and entities with proven experience in assisting women and girls who are victims of sex trafficking, particularly those who participate in public programs for their assistance and protection."[54] As in previous cases, the priority objectives are to:

- Provide adequate information to women and girls about their rights, services, and resources.
- Establish the criteria for a correct evaluation of the needs of the victim that allow adequate assistance.
- Establish indicators that facilitate the identification of women victims of sex trafficking.
- Define the participation of organizations and entities with proven experience in assisting victims of trafficking.
- Establish the mechanisms for systematized coordination among the organizations and/or institutions involved in the protocol.

Navarra took an important step against prostitution and sexual exploitation in 2018 when the parliament approved Law 3/2018 of April 19, which modified the Provincial Law 14/2015.[55] This action marked a milestone in the regional legislation on human trafficking, making it possible for women in a situation of prostitution to be recognized in Navarra as victims of sexist violence. It gave these women access to all the resources the law provided. In addition, the law ensures that no public entity that publishes prostitution advertisements can receive public subsidies since they incite gender-based violence. The law considers that these advertisements possess a clear sexist content. A newspaper in Navarra could earn about €250,000 a year with advertisements of this nature.

On September 22, 2020, the Board of Spokespersons of the Parliament of Navarra approved an institutional declaration on the International Day against Trafficking and Sexual Exploitation of Women and Girls. All political parties voted in favor of the declaration, which stated that "the parliament of Navarra defends a social model that fights for the disappearance of the causes that force women to be prostituted because of the feminization of poverty and male demand. We must act to eradicate those causes and act on the consequences. The sexual exploitation of these women is incompatible with the social model of equality, respect for the dignity of people, and defense of the human rights of women and girls."[56]

A year later, in February 2021, the Navarra Women's Platform for the Abolition of Prostitution (PNAP) called for a law in parliament. PNAP asked for a review of the apartments where prostitution was practiced and the advertising that promotes it. The platform proposed that an abolitionist law be applied in Navarra because "institutions can implement this legislation through policies."[57] Rosario Carracedo from the State Platform of Women for the Abolition of Prostitution (PAP) and representatives of PNAP appeared before the Navarran government department of the Presidency, Equality, Civil Service, and Interior Commission of the Parliament of Navarra. They presented a Proposal for the Abolitionist Organic Law of the Prostitution System (LOASP) prepared by members of the feminist movement and presented publicly three months earlier, in November 2020.

As Carracedo pointed out, this law only requires the minimum since "even well into the twenty-first century, there are still too many places where it is considered acceptable for women to be raped for pay." Carrecedo added that "a society committed to human rights cannot consent to an activity whose economic benefits are derived from the sale and exposure of women."[58] Carracedo pointed out that this type of violence "has perpetrators, and they are 99.99 percvnt men,"[59] so "it cannot be validated and accepted by the culture, the media, and public authorities." She stated that "the lack of action against prostitution normalizes the practice."[60]

For her part, Yolanda Rodríguez (author of one of the chapters in this book) has pointed out that this proposal should lead to the inspection of apartments where prostitution is practiced. The proposal also states that permits for additional locations should not be granted and that advertising aimed at tourists in local publications should be reviewed. The proposal encourages collaboration with Skolae, the co-education program for the sexual education of minors of the government of Navarra. Finally, it proposes blocking online pornography, which can be accessed by minors.[61]

The position of Basque society toward prostitution is progressively abolitionist. In 2022, a study coordinated by Carmen Meneses of the University of Deusto and the Pontifical University of Comillas and published by the Emakunde Institute under the title "Trafficking in women and girls for sexual exploitation in the Basque Country" denounces trafficking in the Basque Country. It brought to light that "they [women] were forced to prostitute themselves every day from noon to midnight."[62] The report points out that there are 1,968-2,308 women in prostitution in the Basque Country. The vast majority are foreigners, some of whom are minors. The report also states that 19 percent of the men in the Basque Country have paid for sexual services.

The study described some of the ways women end up in prostitution. One case described how "recruitment took place through voodoo, a method generally used in Nigeria to recruit women for sexual exploitation in Europe. The women were brought before a shaman, who extracted hair from their scalps and blood from their fingertips. The hair and blood were placed in jars. The women were told that the jars would be broken if they did not pay back the 30,000 euros spent on their journey to Europe. In this culture, the broken bottle represents the death of the person.

The journey took the women through various African countries until they arrived in Italy, traveled to France, and eventually, to the city of Bilbao. During their transit through Africa, they crossed territories controlled by the terrorist group Boko Haram, an ISIS-aligned jihadist group based in Nigeria. The women suffered many hardships during their journey through the desert. After sailing across the Mediterranean in inflatable boats, one group of women was aided by Italian authorities and taken to a center that housed ninety-two immigrants. One of the victims received a message via Facebook from a member of the organization whom she did not know, informing her that she had to arrive in Spain with the other victims. One of the journey organizers appeared in Italy, forcing the women to make the trip to Bilbao. Once there, the women were required to pay off their "debt" of 30,000 euros. Their captors used threats, physical violence, and even sexual assault to keep the women in line. They were forced to prostitute themselves every day of the week from noon to midnight. All the proceeds from the prostitution went to their captors. The women hardly received enough money to meet their basic needs and relied on begging in the streets to survive. One of the victims managed to reach the offices of Ertzaintza, the autonomous police force of the Basque Country. She was able to file a complaint, prompting one of the two leaders of the organization to escape to Germany with another victim. They were readily located thanks to police cooperation between the two countries."[63] This case is just one of many stories collected in the report.[64]

The sad reality of prostitution in the Southern Basque Country today is that it is neither legal nor illegal. It continues to be practiced on the streets, in apartments, and in brothels. It is marketed increasingly on the internet, to the detriment of prostituted persons, who find themselves in a situation of serious vulnerability.

In the Northern Basque Country, prostitution was abolished when the purchase of sex was declared illegal in the French Republic under the law of April 13, 2016. This law aimed to increase the resources available for combatting prostitution and supporting prostituted women.[65] The French law successfully implemented the paradigm shift promoted by the Swedish model under which the client and the organizers of human trafficking networks are penalized instead of the prostituted women. They are considered victims of the system. All institutions and associations agree that the law has decreased the number of users for this type of service. However, out of a total of 40,000 prostituted women, only 161 women have completed the program provided by law to abandon prostitution entirely. Senator Annick Billon, chairwoman of the women's rights delegation, confirmed that the law represents "a considerable advance, a paradigm shift, but its implementation has not lived up to our hopes."[66]

The debate among European administrations for the best way forward focus on four major models:

- The Russian model of prohibition, which prevails in most Eastern European countries (Russia, Lithuania, Belarus, Moldova, Ukraine, Romania, Serbia, Montenegro . . .), simply prohibits the practice of prostitution and punishes both the prostituted women and those who organize the networks.
- The regulatory model, which under various variants prevails in much of Central Europe (Germany, Holland, Switzerland, Austria, Hungary . . .), establishes prostitution regulation systems.
- The abolitionist model, which prevails above all in the Nordic countries (Iceland, Norway, Sweden, Ireland) and now in France, prohibits sexual exploitation but does not punish prostituted women.
- Finally, some countries have not regulated prostitution at all, leaving the people who practice prostitution in a state of legal limbo. Such is the case in the United Kingdom, Finland, the Spanish state, Portugal, Italy, Poland, Bulgaria, Macedonia, the Czech Republic, Slovakia, and Bosnia Herzegovina. The Basque Country is therefore situated halfway between the lack of regulation in the south and abolitionism in the north.

Whether to move toward abolitionist legislation, such as that of Sweden or France, which criminalizes the use and organization of prostitution but not its exercise, or whether it should be regulated as in Switzerland or the Netherlands, countries in which it is legal, began to be publicly debated in Spain in the spring of 2022. The "only yes is yes" bill was put to a vote in the Madrid Congress of Deputies. In the end, the law was passed without the mention of prostitution.[67] Looking at the Swedish model offers some hope for the future. According to Kajsa Wahlberg, head of the Swedish police's human trafficking unit, the abolitionist law has worked. According to data from the Swedish Institute, ten years after it became law, the number of people paying for sex has fallen from 13.6 percent to less than 8 percent of the population.[68] We may see a similar law implemented in the Spanish Basque Country in a few years.

REFERENCES

Aguinaga, Iban, "La Plataforma por la Abolición de la Prostitución urge en Navarra a no dar licencias a puticlubs," EFE, Pamplona, February 2, 2021.

"Aprobada una declaración contra la explotación sexual," Navarra Television, September 21, 2020.

Ayuso, Silvia, "Tras cinco años de ley contra la prostitución en Francia, solo 161 mujeres han dejado la calle," El Pais, Paris, April 13, 2021.

Davila, Pilar; Månsson, Axel-Sven, "Simposio Internacional sobre prostitución y tráfico de mujeres con fines de explotación sexual," Madrid, June 2000.

El fenómeno de la prostitución femenina en Donostia, Servicio municipal para la mujer del Ayuntamiento de Donostia, Donostia, 1990.

"El Gobierno vasco incluye la prostitución en su ley de Espectáculos Públicos y Actividades Recreativas," *Público*, Madrid, November 21, 2018.

Galán, Lola, "Más de cien países sellan en Sicilia el primer convenio de la ONU contra las mafias," *El País*, Palermo, December 13, 2000.

Gil, Lorena, "Apenas un 3% de las 1.820 prostitutas que ejercen en Euskadi ofrecen sexo en la calle," *El Correo*, Bilbao, January 10, 2008.

Hernández Velasco, Irene, "Un millón de hombres al día va de prostitutas," *El Mundo*, December 27, 1996.

Jornadas sobre prostitución 1997. Jornadas organizadas por Askabide los días 12 y 13 de diciembre de 1997 en Bilbao. Askabide, Bilbao, 1997.

Kojima Hoshino, Satoko, "Mapa sobre la prostitución y la trata en Navarra", Acción Contra la Trata, Iruñea-Pamplona, April 24, 2019.

"La prostitución ejercida por las mujeres en la Comunidad Autónoma del País Vasco," Emakunde—Instituto Vasco de la Mujer, Vitoria-Gasteiz, 2002.

Las Heras, A.; Biurrun, J., *La prostitución femenina en Donostialdea*, Diputación Foral de Gipuzkoa, Departamento de Servicios Sociales, Donostia, 1998.

"Las instituciones vascas reforzarán su coordinación para combatir la trata de mujeres y niñas," *Europa Press Euskadi*, September 22, 2021.

"La prostitución se cae del catálogo vasco de actividades recreativas, que sí acepta las eróticas," Cadena SER, Gasteiz, February 5, 2019.

Martín Plaza, Ana, " La prostitución en España: cuántos hombres pagan por sexo y qué zonas concentran una 'oferta' cada vez más digital,'" DatosRTVE, May 26, 2022.

Ordenanza Local sobre Establecimientos públicos dedicados a la prostitución, Administración Local del territorio histórico de Bizkaia, Boletín Oficial de Bizkaia, No. 105, June 14, 1999.

Paredes, María, " La mentira de OnlyFans: proxenetas digitales pagan hasta 400 euros al mes por sustituir a modelos," *El Español*, Madrid, July 2, 2022.

Rioja Andueza, Iker, "Marcha en Bilbao contra la trata de personas para la prostitución," elDiario.es, June 23, 2022.

Roldan, Asun; Ormaetxea, Koro; Astrain, Kepa, et al., "El oficio de la prostitución en Navarra: estigmas y modo de vida," Programa de Atención Socio-Sanitaria a mujeres que trabajan en la prostitución, Osasunbidea, March 2003.

Sahuquillo, María R., "Prohibido pagar por sexo en Suecia, Francia y otros seis países: El modelo nórdico, que castiga al cliente para luchar contra las redes y el proxenetismo, cobra fuerza," Madrid, April 21, 2016.

"Se ha presentado la Ley Orgánica Abolicionista del Sistema Prostitucional en el Parlamento de Navarra," PNAP, Iruñea-Pamplona, February 2, 2021.

NOTES

1   "La prostitución ejercida por las mujeres en la Comunidad Autónoma del País Vasco (Prostitution exercised by women in the Autonomous Community of the Basque Country)," Emakunde—Instituto Vasco de la Mujer, Vitoria-Gasteiz, 2002, 11.

2   Roldan, Asun; Ormaetxea, Koro; Astrain, Kepa, et al., "El oficio de la prostitución en Navarra: estigmas y modo de vida (The trade of prostitution in Navarra: stigmas and way of life)," Program for Social and Health Care for women who work in prostitution, Osasunbidea, March 3, 2003. https://www.media-diversity.org.

3   It is very difficult to determine the number of women who practice prostitution. According to the report on the situation of human trafficking for the purpose of sexual exploitation of the Intelligence Center against Organized Crime (CITCO) of the Ministry of the Interior of the Spanish state, in 2012, there were approximately 45,000 prostituted women. The Comprehensive Plan to Combat Trafficking in Women and Girls for Sexual Exploitation (2015-2018) of the Ministry of Health recognized this data as accurate. However, sociologist Antonio Ariño has pointed out that the figure of 45,000 only includes women who are victims of sex trafficking. In reality, 100,000 to 120,000 women practice prostitution in the Spanish state.

4   Davila, Pilar; Månsson, Axel-Sven, "Simposio Internacional sobre prostitución y tráfico de mujeres con fines de explotación sexual (International Symposium on Prostitution and Trafficking of Women for the Purpose of Sexual Exploitation)," Madrid, June 2000.

5   Hernández Velasco, Irene, "Un millón de hombres al día va de prostitutas (A million men a day are prostitutes)," *El Mundo*, December 27, 1996, 26.

6   Gil, Lorena, "Apenas un 3% de las 1.820 prostitutas que ejercen en Euskadi ofrecen sexo en la calle (Barely 3% of the 1,820 prostitutes who work in Euskadi offer sex on the street)," *El Correo*, Bilbao, January 10, 2008. https://www.elcorreo.com/vizcaya/20080110/pvasco-espana/apenas-prostitutas-ejercen-euskadi-20080110.html.

7   Gil, Lorena, "Apenas un 3% . . . ," *El Correo*, 2008.

8   Roldan, Asun; Ormaetxea, Koro; Astrain, Kepa, et al. "El oficio de la prostitución en Navarra: estigmas y modo de vida (The trade of prostitution in Navarra: stigmas and way of life)," Program for Social and Health Care for women who work in prostitution, Osasunbidea, March 2003. https://www.media-diversity.org.

9   Gil, "Apenas un 3% . . . ," *El Correo*, 2008.

10   Gil, "Apenas un 3% . . . ," *El Correo*, 2008.

11   Gil, "Apenas un 3% . . . ," *El Correo*, 2008.

12   Gil, "Apenas un 3% . . . ," *El Correo*, 2008.

13   "2.000 mujeres ejercen la prostitución en Euskadi (2,000 women practice prostitution in Euskadi)," Begirada.org, September 23, 2019. https://begirada.org/art/20926/

unas-2000-mujeres-ejercen-la-prostitucion-en-euskadi-y-17-han-sido-identificadas-como-victimas-de-trata.

14 "La prostitución ejercida por las mujeres en la Comunidad Autónoma del País Vasco (Prostitution exercised by women)," Emakunde—Instituto Vasco de la Mujer, Vitoria-Gasteiz, 39.

15 Martín Plaza, Ana, "La prostitución en España: cuántos hombres pagan por sexo y qué zonas concentran una 'oferta' cada vez más digital (Prostitution in Spain: how many men pay for sex and which areas concentrate an increasingly digital 'offer')," DatosRTVE, May 26, 2022. https://www.rtve.es/noticias/20220526/radiografia-prostitucion-espana/2351461.shtml

16 This data coincides with that provided by Pilar Dávila and Axel-Sven Månsson. Martín Plaza, Ana, "La prostitución en España: cuántos hombres pagan por sexo y qué zonas concentran una 'oferta' cada vez más digital (Prostitution in Spain: how many men pay for sex and which areas concentrate an increasingly digital 'offer')," DatosRTVE, May 26, 2022. https://www.rtve.es/noticias/20220526 /radiografia-prostitucion-espana/2351461.shtml *See also*, Dávila, Pilar; Månsson, Axel-Sven, "International Symposium on Prostitution and Trafficking of Women for the Purpose of Sexual Exploitation," Madrid, June 2000.

17 Garrote, Gorrotxategi, Beñat, "En 2022, la prostitución se desplaza de clubes a pisos por la pandemia (In 2022, prostitution moves from clubs to flats due to the pandemic)," SER Radio Bilbao, June 23, 2022. https://cadenaser.com/euskadi/2022/06/23/la-prostitucion-se-desplaza-de-clubes-a-pisos-por-la-pandemia-radio-bilbao/.

18 This data is what provides the diagnosis of Doctors of the World Navarra in 2017. https://www.medicosdelmundo.org/file/45498/download?token=kDIPRbNf.

19 Llorens, Jordi, "Retrato robot de la prostitución en Euskadi: mujer de 25 años que trabaja en piso particular (Robot portrait of prostitution in the Basque Country: 25-year-old woman who works in a private flat)," *Basque Chronicle*, February 13, 2022. https://www.cronicavasca.com/sociedad/pandemia-desgrafica-rastro-prostitucion-increases-vulnerability-women_601704_102.html.

20 Domínguez, José, "El alquiler sigue al alza en Bizkaia y supera los 700 euros de media (Rent continues to rise in Bizkaia and exceeds 700 euros on average)," *El Correo*, July 1, 2022. https://www.elcorreo.com/sociedad/precio-alquiler-euskadi-700-euros-media-20220701112621-nt.html.

21 "La prostitución ejercida por las mujeres en la Comunidad Autónoma del País Vasco," Emakunde—Instituto Vasco de la Mujer, Vitoria-Gasteiz, 26.

22 Roldan, Asun; Ormaetxea, Koro; Astrain, Kepa, et al. "El oficio de la prostitución en Navarra: estigmas y modo de vida (The trade of prostitution in Navarra: stigmas and way of life)," Program for Social and Health Care for women who work in prostitution, *Osasunbidea*, March, 2003. https://www.media-diversity.org.

23 Martín Plaza, " La prostitución en España . . . ," DatosRTVE, May 26, 2022. https://www.rtve.es/noticias/20220526/radiografia-prostitucion-espana/2351461.shtml

24 "La prostitución ejercida por las mujeres en la Comunidad Autónoma del País Vasco," Emakunde—Instituto Vasco de la Mujer, Vitoria-Gasteiz, 32.

25 Javier Guillenea, "Aumentan las mujeres que ejercen la prostitución en Euskadi por su cuenta (Women who engage in prostitution in the Basque Country on their own are increasing)," *El*

Diario Vasco, June 23, 2022. https://www.diariovasco.com/sociedad/aumentan-mujeres-ejercen-prostitutcion-euskadi-20220623200733-nt.html.

26 "2.000 mujeres ejercen la prostitución en Euskadi (2,000 women practice prostitution in Euskadi)," Begirada.org, September 23, 2019. https://begirada.org/art/20926/unas-2000-mujeres-ejercen-la-prostitucion-en-euskadi-y-17-han-sido-identificadas-como-victimas-de-trata.

27 Kojima Hoshino, Satoko, "Mapa sobre la prostitución y la trata en Navarra (Map on prostitution and trafficking in Navarra)," Action Against Trafficking, Iruñea-Pamplona, April 24, 2019. https://accioncontralatrata.com/2019/05/08/mapa-sobre-la-prostitucion-y-la-trata-en-navarra/.

28 Guillenea, "Aumentan las mujeres que ejercen la prostitución en Euskadi por su cuenta (Women who engage)," *El Diario Vasco,* June 23, 2022. https://www.diariovasco.com/sociedad/aumentan-mujeres-ejercen-prostitutcion-euskadi-20220623200733-nt.html.

29 "Igualdad no ve "apropiada" la norma de Justicia para abolir la prostitución (Equality does not see the Justice norm to abolish prostitution as 'appropriate')," *La Vanguardia,* Barcelona, May 24, 2022. https://www.lavanguardia.com/vida/20220524/8289437/igualdad-ve-apropiada-norma-justicia-abolir-prostitucion.html.

30 Llorens, Jordi, "Retrato robot de la prostitución en Euskadi: mujer de 25 años que trabaja en piso particular (Robot portrait of prostitution in the Basque Country: 25-year-old woman who works in a private flat)," *Basque Chronicle,* February 13, 2022. https://www.cronicavasca.com/sociedad/pandemia-desdibuja-rastro-prostitucion-aumenta-vulnerabilidad-mujeres_601704_102.html.

31 Roldan, Asun; Ormaetxea, Koro; Astrain, Kepa, et al. "El oficio de la prostitución en Navarra: estigmas y modo de vida (The trade of prostitution in Navarra: stigmas and way of life)," Program for Social and Health Care for women who work in prostitution, *Osasunbidea,* March, 2003. https://www.media-diversity.org.

32 Llorens, "Retrato robot de la prostitución . . . ," *Basque Chronicle,* February 13, 2022.

33 Llorens, "Retrato robot de la prostitución . . . ," *Basque Chronicle,* February 13, 2022.

34 https://www.askabide.org/.

35 Kojima Hoshino, Satoko, "Mapa sobre la prostitución y la trata en Navarra (Map on prostitution and trafficking in Navarra)," *Action Against Trafficking,* Iruñea-Pamplona, April 24, 2019. https://accioncontralatrata.com/2019/05/08/mapa-sobre-la-prostitucion-y-la-trata-en-navarra.

36 Paredes, María, "La mentira de OnlyFans: proxenetas digitales pagan hasta 400 euros al mes por sustituir a modelos (The OnlyFans lie: digital pimps pay up to 400 euros a month to replace models)," *El Español,* Madrid, July 2, 2022. https://www.elespanol.com/reportajes/20220702/mentira-onlyfans-proxenetas-digitales-eur-mujeres-modelos/682431929_0.html.

37 Llorens, " Retrato robot de la prostitución . . . ," *Basque Chronicle,* February 13, 2022.

38 Martín Plaza, " La prostitución en España . . . ," DatosRTVE, May 26, 2022.

39 "La prostitución ejercida por las mujeres en la Comunidad Autónoma del País Vasco," Emakunde—Instituto Vasco de la Mujer, Vitoria-Gasteiz, 26.

40 Organic Law 10/1995, of November 23, of the Penal Code.

41 "La prostitución ejercida por las mujeres en la Comunidad Autónoma del País Vasco," Emakunde—Instituto Vasco de la Mujer, Vitoria-Gasteiz, 27-30.

42 Galán, Lola, "Más de cien países sellan en Sicilia el primer convenio de la ONU contra las mafias (More than a hundred countries seal the first UN agreement against mafias in Sicily)," *El País*, Palermo, December 13, 2000. https://elpais.com/diario/2000/12/13/internacional/976662008_850215.html

43 Palermo Protocol. https://www.refworld.org.es/pdfid/50ab8f392.pdf.

44 Organic Law 4/2000, of January 11, on the rights and freedoms of foreigners in Spain and their social integration. https://www.boe.es/buscar/act.php?id=BOE-A-2000-544.

45 "La prostitución ejercida por las mujeres en la Comunidad Autónoma del País Vasco," Emakunde—Instituto Vasco de la Mujer, Vitoria-Gasteiz, 27-30.

46 New strategy to combat human trafficking (2021-2025). https://europedirectsevilla.us.es/2021/04/15/nueva-estrategia-de-lucha-contra-la-trata-de-seres-humanos/.

47 A comprehensive plan to combat trafficking in women and girls for sexual exploitation 2015-2018. Ministry of Health, Social Services, and Equality. https://violenciagenero.igualdad.gob.es/planActuacion/planContraExplotacionSexual/docs/Plan_Integral_Trata_18_Septiembre2015_2018.pdf.

48 "El Gobierno vasco incluye la prostitución en su ley de Espectáculos Públicos y Actividades Recreativas (The Basque Government includes prostitution in its law on Public Shows and Recreational Activities)," Público, Madrid, November 21, 2018. https://www.publico.es/politica/gobierno-vasco-incluye-prostitucion-ley-espectaculos-publicos-actividades-recreativas.html.

49 "El Gobierno vasco incluye la prostitución en su ley de Espectáculos Públicos y Actividades Recreativas (The Basque Government includes prostitution in its law on Public Shows and Recreational Activities)," Público, Madrid, November 21, 2018. https://www.publico.es/politica/gobierno-vasco-incluye-prostitucion-ley-espectaculos-publicos-actividades-recreativas.html.

50 "La prostitución se cae del catálogo vasco de actividades recreativas, que sí acepta las eróticas (Prostitution falls out of the Basque catalog of recreational activities, which does accept erotic ones)," *Cadena SER*, Gasteiz, February 5, 2019. https://cadenaser.com/emisora/2019/02/05/ser_vitoria/1549393129_526835.html.

51 "Las instituciones vascas reforzarán su coordinación para combatir la trata de mujeres y niñas (Basque institutions will strengthen their coordination to combat trafficking in women and girls)," *Europa Press Euskadi*, September 22, 2021. https://www.europapress.es/euskadi/noticia-instituciones-vascas-reforzaran-coordinacion-combatir-trata-mujeres-ninas-20210922133538.html.

52 Interinstitutional agreement for effective coordination in the care and prevention of violence against women, Iruñea-Pamplona, December 17, 2010. https://www.navarra.es/NR/rdonlyres/62AE8108-EE31-4EED-8AAE-B5C456BD6CDA/170548/AcuerdoInterinstitucionalparalacoordinaci%C3%B3nefectiv.pdf

53 Provincial Law 14/2015, of April 10, to act against violence against women. http://www.lexnavarra.navarra.es/detalle.asp?r=35670#Ar.3.

54 Coordination and action protocol with women and girls who are victims of trafficking for

the purpose of sexual exploitation, Navarro Institute for Equality–Government of Navarra, Iruñea-Pamplona, December 2, 2016, 17. https://www.igualdadnavarra.es/imagenes/documentos/-22-f-es.pdf?ts=20200407092132.

55 Provincial Law 3/2018, of April 19, for the modification of Provincial Law 14/2015, of April 10, to act against violence against women. http://www.lexnavarra.navarra.es/detalle.asp?r=50087.

56 "Aprobada una declaración contra la explotación sexual (A declaration against sexual exploitation approved)," Navarra Television, September 21, 2020. https://www.navarratelevision.es/noticia/ZE7734A27-95DF-1AEF-CE72F2F2411C04B6/202009/aprobada-una-declaracion-contra-la-explotacion-sexual.

57 Aguinaga, Iban, "La Plataforma por la Abolición de la Prostitución urge en Navarra a no dar licencias a puticlubs (The Platform for the Abolition of Prostitution urges in Navarra not to license brothels)," *EFE*, Pamplona, February 2, 2021. https://www.noticiasdenavarra.com/actualidad/sociedad/2021/02/02/plataforma-abolicion-prostitucion-pide-ley/1116963.html.

58 "Se ha presentado la Ley Orgánica Abolicionista del Sistema Prostitucional en el Parlamento de Navarra (The Organic Law Abolitionist of the Prostitutional System has been presented in the Parliament of Navarra)," PNAP, Iruñea-Pamplona, February 2, 2021. https://leyabolicionista.es/ley-abolicionista-sistema-prostitucional/.

59 "Se ha presentado la Ley Orgánica Abolicionista del Sistema Prostitucional en el Parlamento de Navarra (The Organic Law Abolitionist of the Prostitutional System has been presented in the Parliament of Navarra)," PNAP, Iruñea-Pamplona, February 2, 2021. https://leyabolicionista.es/ley-abolicionista-sistema-prostitucional/.

60 "Se ha presentado la Ley Orgánica Abolicionista del Sistema Prostitucional en el Parlamento de Navarra (The Organic Law Abolitionist of the Prostitutional System has been presented in the Parliament of Navarra)," PNAP, Iruñea-Pamplona, February 2, 2021. https://leyabolicionista.es/ley-abolicionista-sistema-prostitucional/.

61 Aguinaga, Iban, "La Plataforma por la Abolición de la Prostitución urge en Navarra a no dar licencias a puticlubs (The Platform for the Abolition of Prostitution urges in Navarra not to license brothels)," EFE, Pamplona, February 2, 2021. https://www.noticiasdenavarra.com/actualidad/sociedad/2021/02/02/plataforma-abolicion-prostitucion-pide-ley/1116963.html.

62 Rioja, Iker, "Un informe denuncia la trata en Euskadi (A report denounces trafficking in Euskadi)," elDiario.es, June 23, 2022. https://www.eldiario.es/euskadi/informe-denuncia-trata-euskadi-obligadas-prostituirse-dias-mediodia-medianoche_1_9110421.html.

63 Rioja Andueza, Iker, "Marcha en Bilbao …," elDiario.es, June 23, 2022. https://www.eldiario.es/euskadi/informe-denuncia-trata-euskadi-obligadas-prostituirse-dias-mediodia-medianoche_1_9110421.html.

64 Rioja Andueza, "Marcha en Bilbao …" elDiario.es, June 23, 2022. https://www.eldiario.es/euskadi/informe-denuncia-trata-euskadi-obligadas-prostituirse-dias-mediodia-medianoche_1_9110421.html

65 Loi française du 13 avril 2016 visant à reinforcer la lutte contre le système prostitutionnel et à accompagner les personnes prostituées, CAP international, Paris, March 2017. http://

www.cap-international.org/wp-content/uploads/2017/04/CAP-brochure-MARS2017FR-WEB2.pdf.

66 Ayuso, Silvia, "Tras cinco años de ley contra la prostitución en Francia, solo 161 mujeres han dejado la calle (After five years of the law against prostitution in France, only 161 women have left the street)," El Pais, Paris, April 13, 2021. https://elpais.com/sociedad/2021-04-13/tras-cinco-anos-de-ley-contra-la-prostitucion-en-francia-solo-161-mujeres-han-dejado-la-calle.html.

67 Martín Plaza, " La prostitución en España. . . ," DatosRTVE, May 26, 2022. https://www.rtve.es/noticias/20220526/radiografia-prostitucion-espana/2351461.shtml

68 Sahuquillo, María R., "Prohibido pagar por sexo en Suecia, Francia y otros seis países: El modelo nórdico, que castiga al cliente para luchar contra las redes y el proxenetismo, cobra fuerza (Paying for sex prohibited in Sweden, France, and six other countries: The Nordic model, which punishes the client to fight against networks and pimping, gains strength)," Madrid, April 21, 2016. https://elpais.com/internacional/2016/04/07/actualidad/1460050306_463588.html.

<h1>Chapter 5</h1>

Social Imaginaries of Prostitution
Transferences in the Circle of Sexual Victimization

Silvia Pérez Freire

The patriarchal contexts in which the different types of sex trade develop in current societies (prostitution, sexual exploitation, sex trafficking), and the divergent judicial-political responses (legalize, tolerate, punish) unequivocally contribute to a sociocultural construct of vague social imaginaries that functions to neutralize any criticism regarding this phenomena. What the so-called first-order observers (social agents directly linked to this social reality: public institutions, legal system and the police, specialized nongovernmental organizations (NGOs), professional experts, client/pimps, and victims) say, do, and narrate constitute diverse social systems, which serve to represent the social imaginaries that enables feedback in the circle of sexual victimization, where victims are vilified and criminals become the victim of sex trafficking. This entrenches patriarchal woman/perverse whore myths, and expunges/transfers the social and individual responsibility of the suspiciously perceived harm and psychological injury resulting from prostitution.

INTRODUCTION

When we speak of prostitution or problematize it, are we speaking of the same thing? In any delimitation of an object under study, the first step is to clearly define the phenomenon to be assessed before determining its dimensions and the profiles of the agents involved. Thereafter, we may proceed to examine, if considered appropriate, the causes and consequences, as well as reaching a consensus on the role of society, and the response and treatment of diverse institutions. Our point of departure sets our sight, as the French anthropologist Alphonse Bertillon noted, "one only sees what one looks at, and one only looks at what is in the mind." That is why what we focus on is what we consider important, while other elements are blanked out from the picture for not being key parts of the issue at hand. A similar perspective is found in social imaginaries theory: by asking questions that are not usually asked when the code of relevance is applied (presence, what stands out), or opaqueness (absence, what is concealed) to a social phenomenon. Juan Luis Pintos (2003) has conceptualized social imaginaries as "socially constructed schemata that guide our perception, provide our explanations, and enable our intervention in what is conceived as reality in different social systems" (2014, 7-8). In other words, precepts guide our action in a specific system.

In terms of prostitution, which is essentially an opaque phenomenon in society (an informal, largely neglected, undisclosed, and socially sanctioned activity), elements tend to be distorted and artificial than in other contexts (legitimized because of their immanence through history, and culturally self-referenced through unreal mythifications derived from male sexual ideology nurtured by literature, cinema, and the mass media, among others). This is applicable to prostitution, where the primary and crucial task (apparently simple) of defining prostitution is considerably problematic, and further confounded when we address other issues that are rarely mulled in discussions on this topic. A feminist premise/maxim is the importance of naming, the need to name ourselves, to name women, assign ourselves a place in history, because what is not named does not exist and is devoured by what is universal, neutral, and masculine. This perspective asserts that the prism from which we view society is biased by the perception of men since there are different implications according to sex in all cultures worldwide that embody sexist "double standards." Thus, in a specific sociocultural context, women and men are judged differently for the same behavior or situation. In relation to prostitution, we should begin by questioning what is almost axiomatic and naturalized, a crucial question that is often overlooked and its significance undermined: Why does prostitution essentially involve women?

In the same circumstances of dire need, vulnerability, or a weighted decision of opportunity, why is there no equivalent number of men who prostitute themselves, or exploit/traffic other men? Although the answer to this question is hardly trivial, whimsical, or inconsequential, discussions on prostitution normally omit this comparative figure, and it is defined by the Royal Academy of Spanish as an "activity of whom maintains sexual relations with people in exchange of money" (RAE 2014), making no reference to the fact that most prostitutes are women (suppliers), and men are mostly the buyers of sex (demanders), including male prostitution. The definition of prostitution of the Royal Academy of Spanish appears to be neutral and objective, but it obscures facts that bias or skew our approach to the analysis and assessment of this phenomenon. We live in the midst of a highly genderized society that transmits an array of connotations linked to gender-mediated power relations and social inequality. Both in real and symbolic terms, prostitution can be regarded as a paradigmatic indicator of the reproduction of inequity between men and women in our societies (Gerda Lerner 2017), which is manifested in the exertion of sexual control over women. Bearing in mind these considerations, perhaps a more appropriate definition of prostitution and its role in society is the description of Victoria Sau (2000, 253):

> Male patriarchal institution whereby an indefinite number of women never get to be distributed to a specific number of men by the collective of men so that they are at the mercy not of one but of all those who wish to have access to them, which is usually mediated by a simple economic compensation.

In this manner, prostitution is placed in the sociocultural context to which it belongs, and judgments are made regarding its role in society. As it is a pre-established institution created to fulfill specific functions (one of which is to guarantee a historically male-legitimated social demand), it is structurally configured through the establishment to perpetuate female sexual subordination (regardless as to whether women want to participate or not).

This chapter aims to undertake a sociological analysis of the phenomenon of prostitution from a social imaginaries and feminist theoretical perspective. Moreover, the results of several recent studies are reviewed concerning agents directly involved in this phenomenon (referred to as first-order operators and/ or observers because of their implication) from several cities across Spain: Vigo, Ourense, Leon, Oviedo, Valencia, Zaragoza, Barcelona, Bilbao, San Sebastian, Madrid, and Seville. Thus, part of the sample was drawn from the results of my doctoral thesis that examined public institutions (political representatives from two major Spanish councils: Valencia and Barcelona; n=3); the legal system and the police (one judge, four prosecutors of the Aliens and Immigration Office, two civil guards, seven national police officers, two work inspectors; n=16); NGOs (n=20); clients/pimps (n=12); and victims (n=12). A total of sixty-seven participants were grouped into three discussion groups, with thirty-two individual interviews, and one group interview. A further part of the sample consisted of statements from other clients from Bilbao and San Sebastian who were part of the research project funded by the Women's Institute of the Spanish Ministry of Equality and undertaken by Vigo University[1], and have been mentioned to take into account the specificity derived from the community to which they belong.

SOCIAL IMAGINARIES AS AN ANALYTICAL TOOL FOR UNDERSTANDING THE SOCIAL SIGNIFICANCE OF PROSTITUTION—SEXUAL EXPLOITATION—SEXUAL TRAFFICKING IN PATRIARCHAL SOCIETIES.

A premise/maxim of the theory of social imaginaries is that what is not named may be as or more important, than what is manifested (in fact, this is usually so). Through discourse analysis (of what is said and not said, in contrast to others) a cosmovision can be developed of the frameworks of signification in which groups and social systems operate in their instituted and institutionalizing dynamics (Humberto Maturana 1985), which generate the precepts anticipating social action. In the words of Juan Luis Pintos: "Imaginaries are linked to the empirical, and its mechanisms, not to people's ideas or beliefs. The question posed is not 'what do people believe?,' but 'what happens to people to believe certain things?' And this happens in specific societies producing certain mechanisms that determine the observability of the observable." (Juan Luis Pintos 2014, 8).

So, why examine the social imaginaries of prostitution? Because it would reveal the "heart" of its contradictions and further our understanding of its immanence in society. Is there an explanation for why something occurred in a "particular way" and not in another? We should bear in mind our entire reality is eminently social, and our individuality is built on the basis of others and the recurrence of our interactions. Through language we express and identify with a particular way of seeing the world, which is why language is a reflection of both the individual and the surrounding world in which one lives. Each social system operates differently and is naturalized in the way it constructs perceptions of reality, which are expressed through communication, and the personal interests of the stakeholder. This underscores that it is not only important how we define prostitution, but also how we name it: Sex trade? Sexual service? Sex worker? The way of naming it expresses a particular viewpoint that assigns social roles, relations, and expectations. Moreover, the judicial treatment of prostitution and its different contexts (legal or not) also has a viewpoint, that of the state, through which groups/systems operate and "self-justify" themselves.

In terms of Spain, prostitution is neither penalized (not an offense), nor acknowledged as a legitimate economic activity (neither as self-employed nor employed labor), making it an illegal activity, with ambiguous and contradictory regulatory bylaws (María Gavilán 2015). Although prostitution is not penalized under the Spanish Penal Code, the behavior of third parties who exploit prostitutes, commonly referred to as pimping, is considered an offense. The de facto stance of public institutions is absolute tolerance to sexual exploitation, and offenses go unprosecuted on the prosecutors' own instructions: circular 5/2011 on the unification of criteria for the specialized action of public prosecutors of the Aliens and Immigration Office states, "there is no coercion in prostitution when the victim voluntarily comes to our country with the intention and knowledge of exercising prostitution," (Official State Gazette of Spain 2011),[2] this implies that being informed of the activity is incompatible with abuse and vitiated consent.

The absence of jurisprudence, the lack of criminal convictions, and numerous bars-clubs run by pimps with plainly visible and recognizable neon lighting scattered throughout Spain amount to sexual exploitation, and highlight the widespread social tolerance of the sex trade in Spain. In this institutional context, sexual trafficking has been an offense since 2010, which only differs to the existing offense of sexual exploitation in that the recruitment of prostitutes underpins the intention to exploit (a process requiring a degree of organization, a characteristic of all businesses, and prostitution is no exception). The comments regarding women of a landlord renting a flat for prostitution are worth noting: [CS2–A thirty-six-year-old man with a partner but no children, landlord of a flat used as a brothel in Barcelona, 2015]:

> . . . they may be voluntary or not, they are brought here by criminal organizations, a large club can't gather a workforce of two hundred women simply by being nice, they have providers, nobody says anything, you can't, that's how it is, that's the reality.

In the definition of sexual trafficking, and its transposition into international law through the renowned Palermo Protocol, relevance/opaqueness is applied given that only certain parts are effectively addressed, but others are omitted in practice. Thus, the stipulation that the trafficking of people involves the recruitment, transport, housing, and reception of people using threats or other forms of coercion (deceit, abuse of power, abuse of vulnerable individuals . . .) with the intention of exploiting them, and any consent given at any stage of the process is legally irrelevant as it effectively constitutes exploitation (the offense of premeditation). In labor law, there is no room for any misunderstandings on what constitutes exploitation, and the law is strictly applied, but things are quite different when it is sexual. The statement of the Prosecutor of the Aliens and Immigration Office acknowledges the procedural incongruence: [FJ3–Provincial Prosecutor of the Aliens and Immigration Office]:

> . . . another thing that is often confused and directly affects prostitution, is that it doesn't matter if they consent, that is, people from Morocco, maybe they are willing to work here twenty hours a day for two hundred euros a month because it's better than what they get back there, but that . . . is an affront to their dignity, so it's not allowed, that is, giving consent is entirely irrelevant, and that's crucial in prostitution, no! Because it's very typical to hear the excuse of she knew she was coming to prostitute herself, or she wanted to prostitute herself.

Similar views were expressed by other operators: directors of the Council Departments of Equality, work inspectors, police, and civil guard. Their discourses concerning this incoherence will be analyzed in greater detail in the following section.

WHAT FIRST-ORDER OBSERVERS SAY, DO, AND EXPERIENCE IN RELATION TO THE PHENOMENON OF PROSTITUTION—SEXUAL EXPLOITATION—SEXUAL TRAFFICKING.

When discerning whether prostitution involves exploitation or not, and/or if sexual trafficking is problematic, public institutions and first-order operators/observers responsible for detecting and identifying these situations intervene differently by adapting to the contexts and precepts that drive their collective and individual actions. Thus, the directors of the Council Departments of Equality declared that council policy was to only intervene in these situations when they received complaints from neighbors (therefore the response was reactive). Both prostitution and sexual trafficking are treated as an incidental or isolated event (narrated as a succession of cases in the mass media), which may lead to "social alarm" associated with situations that are the consequences of this phenomenon, without examining either the causes or treatment of the specific situation of the woman. The approach to this problematic issue is what Concha Fagoaga (1994) has termed in the mass media a "synchronic cut-off of reality" (news stories decontextualized from the events and incidents that motivate prostitution). In practice, this leads to unplanned and haphazard council interventions often designed to conceal social problems (face-saving cosmetic surgery where reality is paralyzed, neglected, and fractured to limit its impact on the community). This is characteristic of so-called street prostitution: when many women gather in certain streets of specific residential areas and cause disturbances in the neighborhood, contradictory council bylaws come into force with law enforcement agencies fining women for soliciting in public places while social services provide the legal assistance to appeal the sanctions:

> A very tense atmosphere in the city, particularly in Ciutat Vella, mainly because of the street prostitution, and the neighbors and business complaining, and because in the mass media, certain mass media turned it into a political debate, so councils passed bylaws, commonly referred to as civil bylaws, regulating communal living in public places which cover a broad spectrum of activities such as begging, drinking in public places, skating or playing on the streets, urinating in the street (. . .), people are demanding a more integrated approach to the issue that cannot be reduced to sanctioning, and fines. [director of Barcelona Council Social Services and Equality Department, IP2]

> It was a negative experience in the sense that we saw it was a totally intimidatory measure against women because we attended to them there, and first we had to make it clear that we would not ask for any information regarding their identity, it was voluntary . . . and on top they were illegal immigrants, imagine it! (putting his head in his hands, shaking his head in negation). [director of Valencia Council Social Services and Equality Department, speaking about the experience of the street approach of the local police force who informed women prostituting of their rights, IP1]

Although law enforcement agencies are fully implicated as they are directly involved in investigating offenses, these systems are permeated by social imaginaries, and with precepts driving their group dynamics. It was not until the year 2010 that people trafficking and similar activities (people trafficking: smuggling people for sexual exploitation) were typified as criminal offenses under the Spanish Penal Code, and ceased to be given a quasi-administrative treatment. Currently, they are considered serious human rights violations (it should be noted, in a context of indifference and absolute tolerance to unprosecuted offenses of sexual exploitation and prostitution that go unquestioned). The assimilation of this fact involves a gradual process. According to data from the Spanish Ministry of Health, Social Services, and Equality, law enforcement agencies registered about 10,000 women in situations of sexual exploitation and/or sexual trafficking in 2014, but estimates of all the different contexts have put the true figure at 100,000-400,000 women prostitutes (Cortes Generales 2007). To adapt to this widespread and overwhelming situation, a "fragmentation of reality" is generated. The police, and civil guards in particular, deal with only a minor part of prostitution: easy convictions, that is, only clear-cut cases of sexual trafficking involving extreme violence are prosecuted. The remaining cases go untreated since victims are not fully aware of the violations to their rights, and their powers to intervene with procedural guarantees are mostly limited. There are striking inconsistencies between the data on sexual exploitation from the Spanish Ministry of the Interior, the number of trials and judicial proceedings, and the data from the Prosecutor's Report for the year 2014: 168 reports of human trafficking offenses; 192 identified victims of sexual trafficking, 1,428 victims of sexual exploitation, and a total of twenty-seven convictions:

> We admit those who are referred to in police reports or other acts provide clear evidence they are victims of false pretenses and deceit, or find themselves in a situation of half-slavery . . . and you do get to hear about that!—[FJ10, National Police, chief of the Aliens and Immigration Operational Brigade]

> But, what can you do about sexual exploitation?, look at the number of clubs there are, we'd have to close all of them if we were to go by the rulebook.—[FJ9: National Police from the Aliens and Immigration Brigade]

> One thing is clear, people do what they're told, if there is no order to attack the clubs, they don't, and that's that.—[FJ6: provincial chief of the Spanish Guards Civil]

Why do I have to accuse the Nigerian guy who lives from trafficking Nigerian women, that Nigerian would be out of business if Spain weren't strewn with clubs whose owners turn a blind eye?—[FJ4: provincial prosecutor of the Aliens and Immigration Department]

[**The victim**]: It's complicated . . . you're not conscious that you are a victim, to try to understand it as . . . it's a bit like being the victim of gender violence.—[FJ3: provincial prosecutor of the Aliens and Immigration Department]

Several circumstances surround the investigation of this offense that are well familiar to other operators working from an alternative perspective (not responsible for prosecuting an offender, but offering assistance to victims), such as NGOs. These entities function in the same way as other operators, i.e., the police and judges and/or prosecutors, who are immersed in this fragmentation of reality, but from different perspectives. NGOs deal with the social aspects of this phenomenon. They lack resources and are unable to intervene in an integrated manner, but publicly denounce the violation of victims' rights and raise social awareness of this phenomenon, in particular among those agents directly involved. Moreover, NGOs directly witness the high levels of institutional corruption since their position of trust with women in situations of prostitution, sexual exploitation, and/or sexual trafficking gives them first-hand knowledge of the sex trade in their country, the people who control it, the conditions of women, and the complicity between pimps, mayors, police, judges, and so forth. The widespread social tolerance to prostitution and sexual exploitation may explain the distortions (alliances and/or complicity) in the ties established in the different contexts in which these agents perform their functions. Nevertheless, the mere existence of the trade of sex for money, compromises, to say the least, their professional duties and responsibilities (behavior that is much more common than is initially thought).

Pimps are people with a lot of power because they deal with people from all of the public institutions: politicians, police, mayors, judges . . . they're all clients, what are they going to do about it?—[FJ9: National Police, Aliens and Immigration Brigade]

> [About police officers' paying for sex] A lot of people, and from all ranks, uh! No, don't be led to believe . . . anyway, they've got a fucking habit of blatantly saying they're from Aliens and Immigration, and they're not, and they have drinks and fuck the whores on the house.—[FJ10 National Police, head of operations of the Aliens and Immigration Brigade]

Hence, it is crucial that social entities raise social awareness on this issue, in particular in terms of the demand for prostitution, which should be addressed seriously by public institutions to thwart the sex trade through exemplary convictions and treatments in cases of institutionalized corruption. The case of the Carioca operation uncovered in 2008 is a good example: five hundred victims of sexual exploitation involved in the city of Lugo, which exposed the criminal network of the sex trade with the collusion of police, civil guards, doctors, work inspectors, government subdelegations, and other institutions. Only just recently the prosecution has reached a plea bargain with the defendants' attorneys on their sentencing.

> Report what? . . . you go to the prosecutor and make a complaint, you go to the police and make a complaint, and then everything gets lost in limbo, and never again. . . . [NGO 1 discussion group][3]

> It was only four days ago that they were male prosecutors, male judges, policemen, all men, all of them were in fact the clients, it's always the same: how can they judge anyone, or try to help these girls if tomorrow they are consuming prostitution? . . . [NGO 1 discussion group]

> Many of the civil guards prosecuted in the Carioca Operation, when the trial is over, and so, they're going to get their jobs back, aren't they? I mean, so what! [NGO 2 discussion group]

Undoubtedly, the first-order operators and/or observers most directly involved in prostitution are the clients/pimps, and the women themselves who live this context, and this greater implication generates a greater reaction in the construction of the precepts driving their actions, as will be discussed in the following section.

THE INVISIBILITY OF CLIENTS AND THE TRANSFERENCE OF RESPONSIBILITY
ONTO WOMEN

In the universe of prostitution, perhaps the least studied and invisible figure
is that of the men who pay for sex. This opaqueness functions at two levels:
in the sexual practice itself (concrete), and in the way it is treated by society and the mass media (abstract). Whether it is in open public spaces,
roadside clubs, or the most private of brothels, there is always an infra-
structure designed to conceal the identity of male clients. Good examples
are the parking areas of roadside clubs with vehicles concealed by fences,
hedges, or walls; or the brothels in buildings and flats with concealed and
isolated spaces to avoid encounters while accessing or during their brief
visits, normally lasting about twenty minutes, with additional fees for more
time, traveling, nights. Furthermore, most roadside clubs are licensed as
fake hotels without any registered "guests," or are flats and business premises masquerading as saunas, massage parlors, and businesses of a similar
legitimate nature. Both the activity and the client are camouflaged. This
opaqueness intensifies with the status assigned to women prostitutes, who
become the focus of sociological analysis and the scrutiny of the mass media
(who they are, how many, what do they do, why they do it, how and where
they do it). Strikingly, clients who oil the sex trade with their demand rarely
come under any scrutiny.

The following brief review of the exclusively quantitative studies on the
clients of prostitution offers some insight as to their profile and sexual practices. The first studies on the behavior of men and paid sex were immersed
in the comparative analysis of sexual habits linked to health surveys on HIV
in Europe (Hubert, Bajos, and Sandfort 1998), and ranked Spaniards as the
highest population paying for sex in the year prior to carrying out the survey
(38.1 percent of male Spaniards stated they had paid the services of a prostitute at least once in their lives). These figures coincide with the 2004 and
2009 surveys undertaken by the by the Spanish National Statistics Office
(INE and CIS) on health and sexual habits in Spain. Moreover, 27.3 percent
and 32.10 percent of men in 2003 and 2009, respectively, stated they had paid
for sex at least once in their lives. The Swedish sociologist Månsson (1998),
who has performed pioneering qualitative studies on this issue in Europe
since the 1970s, has concluded that the behavior of clients is legitimized in a
scenario of immunity and control that is constructed through the social deg-
radation of women in situations of prostitution. Likewise, other researchers

have concluded there is no specific sociodemographic profile of men who pay for sex, and the tendency is to speak of different discursive profiles of chauvinistic behavior.

As for the interviews performed in the previously mentioned field studies in several cities across Spain, clients expressed a naturalness to men paying for sex. Businesses involved in prostitution should be considered a "public service" (legalized), with sexual trafficking being dismissed as a tall story, a fantasy of women who only want to make you feel sorry so they can get more money for what they do. The total disconnection expressed in the discourse of these clients is channeled in two directions: against women (for whom they have no empathy), or in terms of the stark realities of the sex trade in which they are immersed (when confronted with the realities of sexual trafficking, they claim it's not their problem, or often dismiss them as unfounded). There are dissidents in those men who are partially in solidarity with the women since they recognize the existing abuse but are conniving with the clientelistic practice and continue to visit these prostitutive spaces. Therefore, in this case we could speak of an adaptive mechanism through which the members of a system normalize the context in which they live, and that is through dissociation from reality.

> Prostitutes normally if . . . they make love, well love, no . . . if they fuck for money, it's crystal clear, but who makes the money, that's something else, no?—[CS4: client of brothel in luxury flat in Zaragoza. A fifty-six-year-old man, single because of an annulled marriage, soldier]

> [As for sexual trafficking] The tears, she shed her tears . . . and so on, but perhaps that's not what really happened.—[S1 in CT6: discussion group of workers in masculinized sectors. A forty-six-year-old married man, client, captain of a fishing boat]

> (laughing) The consumption, the consumption—it's like . . . it's like, let's see, I don't like it . . . I mean, what they're for me is they're very respectable, I don't like to hear when they say . . . they look down on them and treat them like dirt, degrade them, and laugh at them, no? It's like, you go and select a sandwich from a machine, and you have sex with her . . . and you forget about everything, you feel satisfied, and you don't have to spend time flirting, drinks, time, 'up' and 'down.' I don't know if that

happens to women, but anyway, the truth is that . . .—[CS5: client of a brothel in a luxury flat in Zaragoza. A forty-year-old divorced male doctor]

Moreover, reconverted clients are driven by the opportunity of owning a very lucrative business in return for a relatively small investment. From the brothels in flats in Zaragoza; CS1: a forty-eight-year-old married man with four children: "because if this chatterbox can do it, anyone can do it" referring to the woman who received him in a brothel he had visited as a client, and defended himself from any questioning on the ethics of his actions by shifting his own responsibility onto women, as expressed in his own words; and CS2: landlord of a luxury flat in Barcelona, a thirty-year-old married man with no children, "It's the law of supply and demand, or is it the law of demand and supply?" referring to cases where pregnant women prostitute themselves mainly on the internet.

In the case of communities such as the Basque Country, there is a traditional culture of sexual segregation in leisure activities (the Txokos are exclusively masculine spaces where a bunch of friends cook, sing, and have a good time together), which may explain why the practice of paid sex is articulated as a resource closely linked to homosociability:

> I've been several times with a bunch of friends, and so, and some of the clients of my previous business . . . ahhh! Once a client took me to an apartment where there were only under-age juveniles . . . I couldn't, I couldn't do it with any of them, it's too heavy . . . I thought about my sisters, about . . . I lost the client, he stopped doing business with me.—[a thirty-year-old single, unemployed man, Bilbao]

The same dissociative mechanism is also used by women in situations of prostitution, but for them it is a survival strategy for coping with the experience of sexual exploitation and/or trafficking. This adaptive process undergoes many modifications according to the circumstances suffered:

> He turned around and looked at me . . . and said: You're not even good for cleaning. You're only good for being a whore.—[VT2: A thirty-two-year-old single Brazilian woman with no children, victim of sexual exploitation and trafficking]

I arrived at Bilbao and a guy picked me up. There were another two girls, and they took us to a club in Asturias. When we arrived, they took us to the office, and one by one they told us we owed them each 3,700 euros . . . and on top of that, they forced us to hand in our return ticket and passport, and told us we were indebted to them, and had no choice but to pay them . . .—[VT8: a thirty-four-year-old single Dominican woman with five children, victim of sexual exploitation and trafficking]

If I were to tell you . . . to listen to these things is easy, but to live the things we lived is very . . . hard! It's very hard! First because we were forced into having sex with the clients, old guys, oh! My God! Dirty old men who . . . we were forced to be with clients, crying, crying . . . and they didn't care, as long as they could satisfy themselves . . . they weren't bothered at all. . . .—[VT1: a twenty-three-year-old single Paraguayan woman with no children, victim of sexual exploitation and trafficking]

Men, in their purest of forms, they assert their male chauvinism, and we even applaud them for it because that's the rules of the game. . . . There are clients who think because they're paying . . . we don't have any feelings, and they can ask us to do everything they want.—[thirty-year-old Cuban woman living in Bilbao, 2012]

A number of these women victims who make formal accusations of sexual trafficking before the courts lack the right to social assistance, or protection during the trial process. Others suffer secondary victimization with no prospects or expectations, occasionally ricocheting back into the world of prostitution.

CONCLUSIONS. PROSTITUTION AS A DEVALUATION OF LIFE TRANSFORMED INTO AN OBJECT.

Prostitution generates polycontextural contexts (Nicklas Luhmann 1998), juxtaposed situations in which social imaginaries are lived, and confer sense to an individual's social action. The "relevance/opaqueness" code (Juan Luis Pintos

2003) can be used to extricate the most outstanding aspects (present), or the blind spots blurring our vision (absent). With the social imaginaries of prostitution, we also socially construct sexual exploitation and sexual trafficking. In this way, relevance (woman: happy and/or depraved whore) and opaqueness (client) become self-referenced. This serves to monopolize critical thinking and ethical issues on this phenomenon, while a few and specifically identified victims of sexual trafficking are used as scapegoats to regenerate social awareness that turns a blind eye and refuses to address the crux of the matter, the fundamental issue of prostitution itself.

Contrary to expectations, this phenomenon has become of unprecedented and unpredictable relevance in the context of sexual liberalization that anticipated its eradication in a near future, but failed to foresee the opposite scenario of it actually expanding and diversifying. Currently, three factors appear to strengthen the system of prostitution: the first, male domination generating a sense of immunity and social connivance (by displaying a type of traditionally chauvinistic hegemonic masculinity); the second, widespread institutionalized corruption (mainly among politicians, the legal system, and the police), and the unwillingness to treat this phenomenon seriously; and third, the transference of responsibility whereby men shift the blame onto women for the institutionalization of prostitution and the naturalized client condition.

Thus, first-order operators and/or observers working in the same context need a substrate of significance to guide and legitimize their collective and individual actions. In the process enabling social systems/groups to function by themselves (even in the face of apparently contradictory actions that provide mutual feedback) transpires what Cornelius Castoriadis (1975) called the unifying social magma that gives sense to its own dysfunctions and explains systemic contradictions. This process is characterized according to the level of implication of its members, and by the type of mechanism in which they are immersed to obtain the significance needed to cope with the social reality they are living.

Thus, local councils produce the so-called "synchronic cut of reality" to decontextualize their actions; law enforcement agencies and NGOs "fragment" (segment) it to operate; and clients/pimps together with the women/victims generate a direct "dissociation with reality" by naturalizing it to cope with it: the former by having paid sex without empathy, and the latter to cope with the experiences they endure.

Figure 1.
Social magma of prostitution in the social systems analyzed

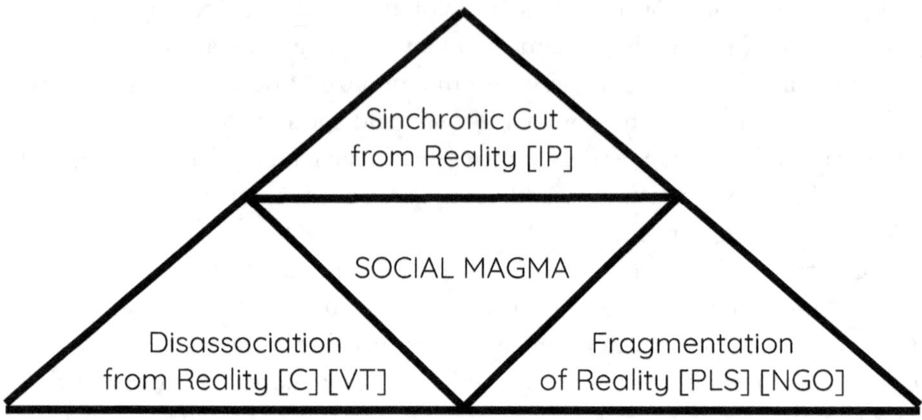

Systems: [IP]: councils (Barcelona/Valencia); [CP]: clients/pimps; [VT]: victims; [PLS]: police and legal system; [NGO]: social entities.

The social hypervisibility of sexual trafficking (a practice that is punished but rarely identified) exorcises the consciousness not assumed in its entire continuum: social tolerance to sexual exploitation and prostitution. The dichotomy, double standards, and contrast between the life experience of women and their clients' lack of empathy, generate the brutally harsh social realities of the prostitutional system.

REFERENCES

Agencia Estatal Boletín Oficial del Estado. Base de datos "Doctrina de la Fiscalía general del Estado." Madrid: BOE, 2011.

Bertillón, Alphonse. "La antropología métrica." Paris, 1909.

Castoriadis, Cornelius. "La institución imaginaria de la sociedad." Barcelona: Tusquets, 1975.

Cortes Generales del Estado. "Informe de la ponencia sobre la prostitución en nuestro país. Aprobada en sesión de la ponencia de 13 de marzo." Boletín Oficial de las Cortes Generales, 367, 13 de abril del 2007.

CIS (Centro de Investigaciones Sociológicas). "Encuesta nacional de salud sexual." Madrid: CIS, 2009.

Fagoaga, Concha. "Comunicando violencia contra las mujeres." Madrid: Editorial Complutense, 1994.

Fiscalía General del Estado. Memoria elevada al Gobierno de S.M. perteneciente al año 2014. Madrid: 2015.

Gavilán Rubio, María. "Delitos relativos a la prostitución y a la trata de seres humanos con fines de explotación sexual. Algunas dificultades en la fase de instrucción." Anuario jurídico y económico Escurialense, n°48, 103-130, 2015.

Gobierno de España. "Plan Integral de lucha contra la trata de mujeres y niñas con fines de explotación sexual." Madrid: Ministerio de Sanidad, Servicios Sociales e Igualdad, 2019.

Hubert, M., Bajos, N. and Sandfort T. "Sexual Behavior and HIV/AIDS in Europe, Comparisons of National Surveys." Londres: University of London, 1998.

INE (Instituto Nacional de Estadística). "Salud y Hábitos sexuales. Las conductas sexuales desde la perspectiva del Sida." Madrid: INE, 2004.

Lerner, Gerda. "La creación del patriarcado." Pamplona: Katakrak, 2017.

Luhmann, Nicklas. "Sistemas sociales. Lienamientos para una teoría general." Barcelona: Anthropos, 1998.

Månsson, Sven-Axel. "El hombre en el comercio sexual." Londres: School of Social Work, 1998.

Maturana, Humberto y Varela, Francisco. "El árbol del conocimiento." Santiago de Chile: Editorial Universitaria, 1984.

Pintos de Cea-Naharro, Juan Luis. Algunas precisiones sobre el concepto de imaginarios sociales. Revista Latina de Sociología, 4, 1-11.

Pintos de Cea-Naharro, Juan Luis. "El metacódigo relevancia-opacidad en la construcción sistémica de las realidades." Revista de investigaciones políticas y sociológicas, 2 (2), 21-34.

Sau, Victoria. "Diccionario ideológico Feminista." Barcelona: Icaria, 2000.

RAE (Real Academia Española). "Diccionario de la lengua española.".Recuperado de: https://dle.rae.es/prostitución?m=form.

NOTES

1   Field study undertaken and documented for my doctoral thesis: "Victimization of sexual exploitation: imaginaries and invisibility," published 2019 by the Spanish Ministry of Equality (all of the interviews were recorded, and transcribed literally: notes were taken after each interview, and later validated with the interviewees; the data gathered was anonymized in compliance with the Spanish Data Protection Law), and the unpublished 2013 research project "Research project final report. Consumption of prostitution in Spain: clients and women (CONPECLIMU)" Exp. Nº2/10, whose head researcher was Águeda Gómez Suárez.

2   Page 33 of the Doctrine of the State General Prosecutor: circular 5/2011, November 2, on the unification of criteria for specialized action of the public prosecutor of the Spanish Aliens and Immigration Office (BOE, 2011)

3   The NGO 1 discussion group was composed of representatives from the following entities: Médicos del Mundo, Abriga, Accem, Faraxa, CCOO-Galicia, Cáritas Vagalume, Adoratrices, Cáritas Alumar. The NGO 2 discussion group was composed of representatives from the following entities: Cáritas Lugo, Aliad Lugo, Ecos de Sur A Coruña, Consorcio de las Mariñas, Oblatas O mencer, UXT-Galicia.

Chapter 6

The New Abolitionism Model

Yolanda Rodríguez Villegas

HISTORY OF ABOLITIONISM: ABOLITIONISM AT THE HEART OF FEMINISM

Feminist tradition has more than three hundred years of longevity in theoretical corpus as well as in practice, if we consider that the first feminists who wrote the vindications of women's rights were Olympe de Gouges with her *Declaration of Rights of Women and Female Citizens* (France, 1791)[1] and Mary Wollstonecraft, with her *Vindication of Women's Rights* (England, 1792).[2] Compiled in these two foundational documents of feminism were the main vindications of women regarding fundamental rights, such as equity of opportunities and freedom, the right to vote and to own private property, the right to access education and to be elected for public office, etc.; rights that, until then, were reserved only for men, and Wollstonecraft herself referred to prostitution as "a humiliating slavery."

Almost half a century had to go by for another woman, Flora Tristán, a French feminist writer and thinker with a Peruvian ancestry, to write a foundational work of abolitionism: *My Walks around London* (1840). In this book, the author "uses experiences lived in the England of her days, in several dates: in 1826, when she sees its affluence without caring for the internal problems; in 1831, when it starts to be possessed by social restlessness; in 1834, when she already is getting the discontent of the middle class and also the pressure of the working class; in 1839, when in London, she finds a deep and lacerating misery among the people and the emergence of an extreme irritation and the general discontent."[3]

In chapter VIII of that book, named "Public Women," Tristan makes a heartbreaking narration of the living conditions of prostituted women in London during the early and middle nineteenth century, and depicts exactly what were, and still are, the two main causes of the existence of prostitution. The first is the impoverishment of women, what we today call the feminization of poverty: girls born in the poor class are pushed into prostitution by hunger. Women are excluded from countryside jobs and when they are not used in manufacturing, they don't have other means of living but domestic servitude and prostitution."[4] The second cause is, of course, the existence of masculine demand:

> I have never been able to see a public woman without being moved by a feeling of compassion for our societies, without feeling despise for its organization and hate for its dominators that, against any modesty, any love for their fellow beings, reduce the creature of God to the lowest grade of abjection. They degrade her to a condition worse than brutal.[5]

And Tristan asks for those men who degrade women in such a way: "Because of that, be this monstrosity imputed to thy social state and be the woman acquitted."[6]

This is one of the core principles of abolitionism: prostituted women are "acquitted" and their rights must be guaranteed, and the pimps and sex buyers must be charged with the crimes that they commit against the women and, therefore, against all women, since if a sole woman or girl is commodified, we all can be.

With good reason, Tristan concluded in her work that "prostitution is the most horrible of the afflictions produced by the unequal distribution of the goods of the world."

The suffragist movement was booming in the late nineteenth century, especially in Great Britain and the United States. The suffragettes centered their demands on the right to vote for women, but also access to education, the right to own property, and custody of children born in marriage in case of separation.[7] Other demands about sexual moral double standards, prostitution, and the age of consent remained secondary.

Suffragette Josephine Butler led the campaign to revoke the Law of Contagious Diseases that "gave the magistrates the power to order a genital exam for prostitutes to seek for symptoms, venereal diseases, and arrest the infected women in a hospital of blockage during three months to be cured." If prostituted women refused to "consent" to this humiliating exam, they would be imprisoned. Prosecution and stigma, once more, would fall on women, who must be healthy to be able to continue being exploited. Butler opposed this law with all her strength and founded the National Association of Women for the Revoking of the Law of Contagious Diseases in 1886.

Additionally, Butler founded the International Abolitionist Federation, originally named "Britannic and Continental Federation for the Abolition of Prostitution," in Liverpool in 1875. Its goals were to fight the state regulation of prostitution in force in all of Europe under the guise of "sanitary laws and laws of prevention of diseases," and to prevent and abolish the trafficking of women for purpose of sexual exploitation. In that moment, incessant trafficking of European women, mainly from Ireland and Eastern Europe (origin of the term, today in disuse, "white [women] slave trafficking") into the thriving Latin American market (mostly in Argentina) was at its peak.[8]

In the late nineteenth and early twentieth centuries, the thriving suffragist movement had adopted the abolitionist vindications. And so, Emmeline and Christabel Pankhurst founded the WSPU (Women's Social and Political Union), whose main goal was to get the right to vote for women, but also integrate the concern of the English feminists about a new ethics of sexuality, away from the puritan Victorian moral, which, nevertheless, allowed men to consume prostituted women. Christabel Pankhurst denounced prostitution in her book *The Great Scourge and How to End It* (1913).[9] Again, a feminist woman would shed light on the true culprits of the existence of the prostitution market: the men as demanders and consumers of women.

That same year of 1913 in Argentina, a fundamental law was passed for the visibility of the existence of trafficked and prostituted women: the 9.143 Law, known as the Palacios Law, for the name of the legislator who wrote and defended it in the Argentinian Senate. This law was passed on September 23, and that date was chosen by the United Nations in 1999 to commemorate the International Day Against the Sexual Exploitation of Women and Children. This law had the purpose of prosecuting the then-called "white [women] slave trafficking" (because it was European women being prostituted in the Argentinian brothels), forced prostitution and pimping, with special attention to the sexual exploitation of minors and the punishment for "roughnecks and pimps." It did not, however, authorize punishment for demanders and consumers. It was centered on identifying and prosecuting pimping and ending the trafficking of white women into Argentina.[10]

In 1921, in the International Convention for the Suppression of Traffic in Women and Children, the term "white [women] slave traffic"[11] was abandoned. This convention was replaced by the Convention for the Suppression of the Traffic in Persons and of the Exploitation of the Prostitution of Others (United Nations, 1949), that establishes one of the fundamental points of abolitionism: that trafficking and prostitution are inseparable, two sides of the same coin. Therefore, if a purpose of democratic societies is to end trafficking inasmuch as this constitutes a crime against women and girls, especially the most vulnerable, this must be started by abolishing prostitution.[12]

> Considering that prostitution and the evil that accompanies it, human trafficking for sexual exploitation, are incompatible with dignity and the value of the human person and jeopardize the welfare and value of the human person, the family and the community.

Deliberately, I have left out of this brief introduction about abolitionism of prostitution what has happened in Spain, a country with a regulationist tradition since 1845 (Regulation of Zaragoza): "Since the first regulations, the Zaragoza of 1845 and the one from 1847 in Madrid, the problem of prostitution is approached from a perspective of public order and health based on the registration of prostitutes in a registry, their mandatory medical examination with a regularity that varied according to the regulations and the compulsory hospitalization in case of contagious disease."[13]

We see this time how the intention of legislators was not ending prostitution nor to provide rights for prostituted women, certainly not; their purpose was to keep them disease-free so the men would not catch venereal infections and wouldn't give their chaste wives and families such diseases.

By the early thirties, the regulationist model had entered, consequently, a crisis, and its days were numbered. In 1932, prominent venereologists and the noted jurist Luis Jiménez de Asúa blocked an abolitionist bill. This project provoked debates in the National Council of Health about the mandatory treatment and the mandatory declaration of diseases. The pressure over regulationism kept building up. In May 1932, abolitionists from Madrid, with the support of psychiatrist César Juarros, would dedicate themselves to propaganda of their ideas for a week, given the slowness of the Ministry of

Govern to order the abolition of regulationism. Most of the medical doctors of the Official Antivenereous Fight, at least in Madrid and the big cities, would openly show themselves as abolitionists. On June 28, 1935, a ruling was issued that suppressed regulationism in Spain, closing a period that started in the early nineteenth century.[14]

If we dive into recent history, we will find a fascinating debate about prostitution. In the General Courts of 1932, during the Second Spanish Republic, a group of male and female members of the Parliament, including Clara Campoamor, exposed that the fight against the prostitutional system should not be made solely on a sanitary approach, with the purpose of stopping venereal diseases, but also with a feminist perspective. They understood that prostitution, as Senator Manuel Rico Avello said, is "absolutely incompatible with human dignity" and, therefore, there is no other option than the simple adoption of an abolitionist theory. The state must avoid, by any means available, promoting and stimulating individual and social prophylaxis; the state must endeavor to set a solid basis for policy and sexual education." Then Senator Cesar Juarros would say, coinciding with the abolitionist path: "Before any other thing, as a first barrier to keep many women from falling into prostitution, we must go to the implementation of postulates such as that of economic freedom, which will allow women to develop with enough material resources."[15]

Thus, the decree issued on June 23, 1935, said in Article 1: "Be the regulation of prostitution suppressed, since it is an activity that is not acknowledged in Spain as a legitimate means of living from the issuance of this Decree."[16]

This debate in the Congress of the Spanish Republic followed a big effort made since the early twentieth century by many Spanish feminists, suffragists, and abolitionists, such as Concepción Arenal, Carmen de Burgos, or Margarita Nelken.[17]

Lastly, we will quote the anarchist group Mujeres Libres [Free Women], founded in April 1936 by Dr. Amparo Poch y Gascón, writer and unionist Lucía Sánchez Saornil, and lawyer Mercedes Comaposada, which also created the magazine *Mujeres Libres* [Free Women] (1936-1938).[18] This group worked on everything related to women: the republic, the civil war, sexuality, education, fashion. They also approached the topic of prostitution; concretely, in issue eleven of this magazine, we can find a text that actions against prostitution are proposed, as a fundamental basis for their liberation from male domination: "both economic liberty and equity, equity of wages, equity of access to means of work of all kinds." In issue five of the magazine, a brief article was published where the creation of "Prostitution Liberatoriums" was proposed. Given the interest and current validity of this text, we reproduce it completely:

> The most urgent venture to achieve in the new social structure is the one of suppressing prostitution. Before we engage in the economy or education, from this very moment, in full anti-fascist struggle, we still have to radically end this social degradation. We cannot think of production, of work, of any kind of justice, while the greatest of slaveries still stands on on foot: the one that disables any dignified living.
>
> The decency of no woman can be acknowledged if we cannot claim it for us all. There is no such wife of someone, sister of someone, partner of someone, while there is a prostitute. Because what supports these titles of honesty, what makes that decency possible, is precisely the prostitute, destined to supply for the respectful vacation granted from the chaste courtship, the healthy lactation, the watched and cared pregnancy of the "decent" woman; the clandestine sexual babbling of teenagers from Christian families; the "affairs" of honest family fathers.
>
> We have to end this swiftly. And it has to be Spain who gives this norm to the world. All Spanish women will have to put ourselves to work on this liberating venture. Not another sham of leagues and speeches "against the 'white [women] slave trade.'" No more somber convents of regretful women. No more passive commiserations from distant women. It is not their problem, but ours, of all women and of all men. While it exists there cannot be an achievable sincerity in love, in affection, in friendship, in comradeship.
>
> We have to hurry in doing what was never done by feminine associations that pretended to emancipate women by organizing some entertaining conferences, some readings of elegant male and female poets and by preparing some typists.
>
> In several locations that we have recently visited it has been brought to our attention, as a great measure, that they had "suppressed" prostitution. When asked how and by what

means this had been achieved, they responded: "Oh, that's those women's problem!" This way, suppressing prostitution is very simple: it is merely leaving some women out on the streets, without any means of living.

Free Women is organizing prostitution liberatoriums, that will begin to work in a brief period. Adequate venues are being destined to this purpose in different provinces, and in those spaces the following plan will be developed:

1. Research and medical/psychiatric treatment.

2. Psychological healing and ethics to promote a sense of responsibility in the students.

3. Vocational orientation and professional training.

4. Moral and material help in any moment necessary, even after becoming independent from the liberatoriums.

Those days, posters will appear on the streets announcing precise directions about information and registration for these liberatoriums.

We expect all working class organizations and women's associations, political parties and all conscious men and women to collaborate in this work, where *Free Women* puts all of its emancipating and constructive enthusiasm.

Free Women. 65 days of the Revolution [July 19 to September 22, 1936].[19]

APPROACHING THE PROSTITUTION SYSTEM: DIFFERENCES BETWEEN PROHIBITIONISM, REGULATIONISM, AND ABOLITIONISM

Until now, we have been reviewing the beginnings of abolitionism, which coincide with those of feminism, and we have only mentioned briefly other approaches to prostitution that have emerged in history and that are still in force: regulationism and prohibitionism.

Prohibitionism

Prohibitionism of prostitution is an approach that considers this activity a felony that is committed, therefore, by all the parties involved; that is, prostituted women as well as demanding men and pimps, are prosecuted. It seeks the eradication of prostitution through the criminal prosecution, even of those considered victims: the very prostituted women.

By considering the prostitute a delinquent, this model doesn't offer alternatives to these women regarding the activity they perform, but instead it tries to eliminate their presence in society, especially in the streets, since it guards the public space.

At a global level, there is no other country that openly declares itself prohibitionist, since this model is often combined with shades of prostitution regulation. Ireland and Malta are close to this model.

Regulationism

In a very brief way, since it is not the goal of this analysis, I will speak here about regulationism, a model that legalizes prostitution, which in some spheres is called "pro-rights" because it centers its efforts on having prostitution acknowledged as a form of work, called "sex work," and prostituted women as "sex workers," while omitting the causes of the existence of prostitution: feminization of poverty (neoliberal capitalism), male demand (patriarchy), and the existence of a huge number of women from impoverished countries available for that demand (racism-colonialism).[20] It also omits consequences that prostitution has for the very prostituted women regarding physical and mental health, something explained by forensic psychologist Laura Redondo in an interview for Médecins du Monde Navarra (Doctors of the World):

- Drug, alcohol, and medication abuse.
- Dissociation.
- Self-blaming and shame.
- Forced pregnancies.
- Forced abortions.
- Sexual violence.[21]

These consequences encompass post-traumatic stress disorder, which psychologist Melissa Farley describes this way:

> Post-traumatic stress disorder occurs when a person has been subjected to overwhelming and inescapable stress. PTSD is a global indicator of the emotional damage against women in prostitution, partly resulting from the way that men use pornography with and against them. The psychiatric diagnoses of PTSD describe mental and physical behaviors of omission,

psychological numbness, social distancing, flashbacks and hyper-stimulated physiological anxiety.[22]

Dissociation, a phenomenon that Dr. Ingeborg Kraus describes with the words of Dr. Michaela Huber, director of the German society Trauma and Dissociation, is depicted in the article as follows:

> To allow strange people penetrating your body, it is necessary to suppress natural phenomena, [such as] fear, shame, disgust, the feeling of oddness, contempt, guilt." Instead of that, women turn on indifference, neutrality, a functional concept of penetration, a redefinition of this action to transform it into a "job" or a "service."[23]

Without forgetting the physical and psychological violence that is intrinsic to prostitution, which is increasing because of the expansion of pornography, the forced pregnancies and abortions, the diverse addictions: alcohol, drugs, medications, shopping… often induced by pimps and buyers, but also resulting from having to "endure" being in prostitution.

Lastly, but not less important, the prostitution system implies consequences for the fundamental rights of human beings. Following Ana de Miguel, we will say that "a society that trivializes, normalizes, and idealizes the prostitution of women is a society that strengthens the roots of human inequity."[24]

Prostitution is incompatible with the equity between men and women and is contrary to the dignity of persons since it gives the message that women, all women, are commodities. Contrary to freedom, a false notion of "free choice" to do with your body whatever you want hides the fact that prostituted women lack freedom to live their lives and sexuality the way they want and desire because they are always subjected to the wishes of others.

Abolitionism

As we have already spoken about abolitionism, and will speak later on, we wish to point to three basic problems:

- Prostitution is considered a practice of constant sexual exploitation. The concept of consent loses relevance, since it is considered nonexistent in prostitution, and trafficking and prostitution are inseparable concepts, as was established in the

UN Convention signed in 1949, because they are incompatible
with the dignity of persons, families, and communities.

- Prostituted women are *never* prosecuted, and they are provided
  with aids such as psychosocial support, education, job opportunities, housing, legal support, etc. Additionally, the rights of
  women survivors of prostitution are guaranteed for all effects.
  In the laws that prosecute violence against women, prostitution
  was considered a form of sexual violence and female victims of
  this violence will be able to access resources in the same conditions of equity as other women.[25]

- Pimping is criminally prosecuted, as well as the demand of
  prostitution, whether by administrative, economic, or criminal
  sanctions. Campaigns of education, training, and sensitization
  to discourage the demand are required and necessary and also
  the need for training professionals on an approach to prostitution with a feminist and gender perspective.

NORDIC MODEL

The implementation of abolitionism as a model for approaching the prostitution system, setting aside the shy approaches of the Second Spanish
Republic, was carried out in 1999 in Sweden, with a law that treated the
different forms of violence against women and included prostitution
among them.

This law is known in Spanish as the "Law of peace for women." One of its
advocates, Gunilla S. Eckberg, describes the Swedish law as follows:

> The *Swedish approach*, that brings the complete criminalization
> of those who are responsible for the exploitation of a great
> number of women and girls (but also men and boys) for the
> purpose of prostitution—traffickers, recruiters, and individuals
> that pay for sexual services—while it is assured that those
> prostituted are not prosecuted, are given access to fully funded
> projects to exit, support, and protection.[26]

This approach was recommended by the European Parliament in 2014 in
its Resolution of the European Parliament, issued on February 26, 2014, on
sexual exploitation and its impact on gender equality (2013/2103(INI), as the
best way to face the trafficking of women and children for sexual exploitation,

that "reveals that some data confirm the dissuasive effect of the Nordic model on human trafficking into Sweden, where prostitution and trafficking has not increased, and that people increasingly support that model, especially the youth, which proves that legislation has provoked a change of attitude."[27]

In the quoted resolution of the European Parliament, it is asserted that:

> Considering that prostitution and forced prostitution are intrinsically linked to gender inequality in society and have an effect on the social position of women and men in society, as well as the perception of relations between women and men and in sexuality.
>
> "States" are exhorted to fund the organizations that work on site with support and strategies for success, to offer innovative social services to victims of trafficking or sexual exploitation, including migrants and persons without papers, to evaluate their individual necessities and risks in order to offer adequate protection and assistance and to apply policies—with a holistic approach and through the various services of the police, migration, health care, and education—intended to help women and minors prone to abandon prostitution, while ensuring that said programs have a juridical foundation and the necessary funding to achieve this purpose; insists on the importance of psychological assessment and the necessary social reinsertion of victims of sexual exploitation; remarks that this process requires time, as well as the development of a life plan that constitutes a valid and believable alternative for the persons that previously exercised prostitution.[28]

The so-called Nordic model, adopted by other countries such as Norway in 2008 and France in 2016, is based on four pillars:

- Discourage demand.
- Decriminalize prostituted women and fight the stigma.
- Guarantee resources and rights for prostituted women.
- Raise awareness, train, and educate on equity all public powers, the media, and citizenry in general."[29]

In addition, in Norwegian law, a very important novelty was introduced: prosecuting the activity incorrectly referred to as "sexual tourism," which is nothing but sexual exploitation outside the borders of one's own country, perpetrated by Norwegian citizens in the most impoverished countries.

TOWARD AN ORGANIC LAW FOR THE ABOLITION OF THE PROSTITUTION SYSTEM
We have titled the chapter "The New Abolitionist Model," however, we have demonstrated that abolitionism is not a new approach, and that it is very closely linked to feminism, as we asserted in the title and as Rosa Cobo Bedia quoted in the first citation: "abolitionism is at the heart of feminism."

And with that premise, and all the feminist history that is behind, the PAP, the State Platform of Women's Organization for the Abolition of Prostitution,[30] a platform with representatives of women's organizations of all the territory, including Euskal Herria, and constituted in 2002, proposed at the end of 2019 the elaboration of an Organic Law for the Abolition of the Prostitution System that could be presented before the government for approval, considering that abolition of prostitution is a right and a pressing duty for the Spanish society.

The core of the encounter in Madrid was "determining the axis and essential proposals for the elaboration of an Abolitionist Law for Prostitution, that must bind together the work of the abolitionist movement in the next year." This bill, according to the developments of the Encounter, "must have an effect on the three axis of the prostitution system: acting against pimping; acting against the demand of prostitution, with concrete measures aimed to the johns/buyers; and resources, integral reparation, and protection of survivors and prostituted women."[31]

After this first contact, the women's organization members of the PAP gathered again, also in Madrid, on February 22, 2020, and the result of that meeting was a proposal of an Organic Law for the Abolition of the Prostitution System (LOASP).

This text was presented to the media, in a summarized version, on March 6, 2020 (a few days before the COVID-19 pandemic lockdown) and that very day, representatives of the PAP filed a request for a meeting with the Spanish government, because, as one of our representatives said: "a progressive government cannot turn its back on women, nor can it remain an accomplice of sexual exploitation."[32]

This is the summarized proposal that the state feminist movement makes to the government.

In the statement of motives, the purpose of the law is clearly set out:

> This law is aimed to abolish the prostitution system and, there-
> fore, to deconstruct the elements that compose and support it:
> the sex industry, johns, and pimps.

The LOASP revolves around three axis:

1. The first axis are women in prostitution, whose rights included are guaranteed in this or any other law aimed to victims of violence against women and a timeframe and scope of application that includes women suffering this violence in our territory, whether they are in it temporarily or permanently, regardless of the moment that it has happened.

2. The second axis is focused in the dismantling of pimping, the industry of sexual exploitation and the activities of pimps; and aims to deactivate the demand of prostitution, since johns constitute an essential element for the survival of this form of violence and exploitation, including the criminal punishment for the johns and pimps, whether they act individually or collectively, and to introduce third-party locative implication, that is, to prosecute those who confine or imprison women to sexually exploit them in closed spaces.

3. The third axis is related to the measures of prevention, detection, education sensitization, and training aimed to general citizens and to those actors directly implied in the dismantling of the prostitution system and the fight against violence toward women: public administrators, judiciary officers, schools, institutes and universities, communication media, social entities, sanitary system, etc.

The law is composed of four chapters:

- The first chapter is about the general principles that sustain the text of the bill and is concentrated on outlining the purpose of the law, its timeframe and scope of application, its goals, the general principles, the definition of basic concepts that conform the prostitution system, as well as the economical resources.
- The second chapter concentrates on implementing the timely measures of prevention, sensitization, and training that must necessarily run through diverse competencies of the public powers that, by their functions, are implied and committed with their application.
- The third chapter "Of the Rights," is dedicated to a portfolio of rights and resources that must be recognized to women in prostitution, notwithstanding the compatibility of them with others that may be provided to assist women victims of patriarchal violence.
- Chapter four is about the public measures of coordination and collaboration between the different entities that must participate in the implementation of the norm.

Several additional provisions have been modified. Among others, the Integral Organic Law Against Gender-Based Violence, incorporating the feminist argument that the kinship or relationship of the man to the woman does not determine if an action can or cannot be qualified as of sexist violence and presents prostitution as simply one more of the modalities of violence that women and girls suffer; the General Law of Advertising, including as illicit the advertising that has as a purpose the direct or indirect promotion, of prostitution, pornography, and other forms of sexual exploitation and commodification of women; the Organic Law for the Protection of Citizen Security, radically excluding prostituted women from any responsibility; the Law of Free Juridical Assistance was adapted to the purpose of giving prostituted women the same frame of protection and access to justice that are currently enjoyed by women subjected to other forms of patriarchal violence; the law regulating the right to association, by sending an institutional order of not helping or funding any organization that promotes prostitution, pornography, or other forms of sexual exploitation, or normalizes prostitution; the Law of Juridical Regimes of the Public Sector and the Organic Law of Judiciary Power, where having been a demander of prostitution is introduced as a cause for abstention and, therefore, of recusal, by considering that johns cannot perform their functions adequately or with due respect for prostituted women.

And two final provisions related to the enforcement of the law: The demand from the feminist movement that our bill is discussed and passed in general courts, so our state can be a place free of johns and pimps and that it will stop exerting institutional violence by being an accomplice to the patriarchal violence that prostitution implies.[33]

ABOLITIONISM IN NAFARROA

In February 2021, representatives of the Navarra Platform of Women for the Abolition of Prostitution appeared in the Navarra Parliament to present a series of arguments that have to do with the quoted regional Law of Violence Against Women that considers prostitution as sexist violence:

> Prostitution and/or sexual exploitation: the practice of having sexual intercourse with other persons in exchange for money. Obtainment of financial benefits or of any other kind with the exploitation of the exercise of someone else's prostitution (including pornographic actions or the production of pornographic material), even with the consent of the prostituted.[34]

And in consonance with the Institutional Declaration approved by the very Navarra Parliament on September 20, 2020, that summarizes as follows:

> The Parliament of Navarra defends a social model that fights for the obliteration of the causes that force women to be prostituted by the feminization of poverty and the male demand, we must act to eradicate these causes and be able to act on the consequences. Sexual exploitation of these women is incompatible with the social model of equality, respect for the dignity of the persons, and in defense of the human rights of women and girls.[35]

In such appearance, the PAP presented a series of demands to the Parliament, which I summarize as follows:

1. Institutional and political support for the passing of the bill of Organic Law for the Abolition of the Prostitution System made by the feminist movement.

2. A study about the dimension of the prostitution phenomena in Navarra that, in all cases, yield data about demand of prostitution and the true dimension of pimping not only on prostituted women.

3. Elaboration of a protocol of actions toward prostitution in Navarra and not only against trafficking for sexual exploitation.

4. Training about what's entailed and represented by prostitution in our society in all fields (police, public prosecution, judicature, social services, health, psychology, law, education, tourism, tourism attention, public transportation, etc.), as well as in the accreditation of women in trafficking and prostitution.

5. Revision of language that normalizes and promotes prostitution in our society in all social spheres to propitiate a change of mentality into real and effective equality between men and women. We ask for a language free of euphemisms, because otherwise an ideology is created that favors a completely patriarchal and neoliberal practice that turns us into commodities and empties us of all human consideration, all our rights.

6. Actions to make progress in the change of the violent models for the relationship between men and women:

- A regular and funded campaign of social sensitization, about what prostitutes, aimed to deactivate and discredit demand of prostitution.

- Workshops for educating in equality where prostitution is approached as a form of violence against women.
- Workshops of prevention of prostitution addressed at girls to avoid their recruitment and the offering of money in exchange for sex that their partners practice, which entails the normalization of prostitution as a job.

7. Actions against pimping in Navarra:

- Revision of the licenses of the premises of clubs, massage parlors, hotels and motels where prostitution exists, with the purpose of permanently closing them whenever that's possible.
- Revision of unlicensed apartments where prostitution takes place under the control and for the profit of third parties.
- Disapproval of licenses for the opening of clubs, apartments, massage parlors, and hotels and motels for prostitution.
- Revision of all the offers of announcements of prostitution on internet forums, flyers on cars and approval of an executive order that during the implementation of the law prohibits advertising of prostitution in the different municipalities of Navarra.
- Revision of the touristic offer that is exposed in the different hotels, restaurants, and bars of the city where advertisements of prostitution are portrayed and spread.

8. Actions against demand:

- Within the Skolae program, the implementation of measures to deactivate the consumption of pornography in population older than eight, since this is the age when, according to experts, children are introduced to the consumption of pornography through the internet.
- Campaigns of social sensitization that deactivate the demand of prostitution, since it represents the sexual submission of women and the lack of their sexual rights, and hold men responsible for the existence of prostitution and trafficking for sexual exploitation.
- The implementation of sanctions for demanders of prostitution (johns) and the notification in the demander's residence.

9. Actions for women in prostitution independent of their administrative situation, their origin or nationality and regardless of them filing or not any report against the prostitution networks:

- Resources for integral intervention aimed at women in prostitution, that give emergency assistance, assistance for housing, shelter, and integral recovery, juridical, social, and psychological assistance, resources to guarantee the safety of the women and their children whenever happens an attempt against their physical or psychological integrity, or whenever they endure threats.
- Resources of comprehensive sanitary assistance in the public health care network.
- Resources to guarantee the assisted and safe return to their home countries if they request it.
- Resources to guarantee the exit from prostitution of those women that request it
- Financial resources, through the concession of a GUARANTEED INCOME.
- Job resources, set in motion through the programs of social employment intervention until achieving full incorporation into the world of employment.

And we demand THAT THE GOVERNMENT OF NAVARRA:

- Urges the government of the Spanish state to process a bill, for the Senate approval, of an Organic Law for the Abolition of Prostitution System and the development of an abolitionist regulation that guarantees the right to Equal Treatment and Opportunities between women and men and that directly acts against the violence that implies the prostitution system in their various forms: prostitution, trafficking, and pornography.
- A comprehensive response for the prostituted women and survivors of prostitution is guaranteed: that they have guaranteed access to their rights and the social resources that prevent the current situation of helplessness and allow their full social and labor incorporation as well as their medical and psychological recovery; and the implementation of all measures needed to deactivate the demand of prostitution and to end networks of prostitution that profit from the exploitation of the most vulnerable women.

REFERENCES

¿Qué es el modelo nórdico?. *Traductoras para la abolición de la prostitución.* https://traductorasparaaboliciondelaprostitucion.weebly.com/blog/que-es-el-modelo-nordico. Accessed on October 9, 2021.

"El Gobierno de Navarra se suma al Día Internacional contra la Explotación Sexual y la Trata de Personas y expresa su firme compromiso en la erradicación de esta violencia contra las mujeres." *Navarra.es.* September 2020. https://www.navarra.es/es/noticias/2020/09/23/el-gobierno-de-navarra-se-suma-al-dia-internacional-contra-la-explotacion-sexual-y-la-trata-de-personas-y-expresa-su-firme-compromiso-en-la-erradicacion-de-esta-violencia-contra-las-mujeres. Accessed on October 9, 2021.

"La PAP ha celebrado en Madrid un Encuentro para avanzar en la organización abolicionista." *AmecoPress. Información para la ligualdad.* December 2019. https://amecopress.net/El-pasado-fin-de-semana-tuvo-lugar-en-Madrid. Accessed on October 9, 2021.

Presentación pública de la ley abolicionista. *Por la abolición de la prostitución.* March 2020. https://aboliciondelaprostitucion.wordpress.com/2020/03/06/presentacion-publica-de-la-ley-abolicionista/. Accessed on October 9, 2021.

Bacchiega, Julia. "Liberando esclavas." Thesis work for graduating as a historian. University of La Plata. 2016. http://sedici.unlp.edu.ar/handle/10915/67733. Accessed on October 9, 2021.

Bernal Triviño, Ana Isabel. "Cuando la República dijo sí a la abolición de la prostitución." *Publico.es.* November 11, 2018. https://www.publico.es/sociedad/abolicionismo-republica-dijo-abolicion-prostitucion.html. Accessed on October 9, 2021.

Castejon Bolea, Ramon. "Las enfermedades venéreas y la regulación de la sexualidad en la España contemporánea." *Asclepio.* Issue LVI-2. 2004. https://asclepio.revistas.csic.es/index.php/asclepio/article/view/45/44. Accessed on October 9, 2021.

Convención Internacional para la Supresión de la Trata de Mujeres y Menores. 1921. https://www.senado.gob.mx/comisiones/desarrollo_social/docs/marco/Convencion_ITM.pdf. Accessed on October 9, 2021.

Convenio para la represión de la trata de personas y de la explotación de la prostitución ajena. 1949. https://www.ohchr.org/sp/professionalinterest/pages/trafficinpersons.aspx. Accessed on October 9, 2021.

De Gouges, Olympe. "Declaración de los derechos de la mujer y la ciudadana." 1791. http://clio.rediris.es/n31/derechosmujer.pdf. Accessed on October 9, 2021.

Eckberg, Gunilla S. "El abordaje sueco de la prostitución: la paz de las mujeres." 2019. Translated into Spanish by Hinaetefaton Tebas. https://traductorasparaaboliciondelaprostitucion.weebly.com/blog/el-abordaje-sueco-de-la-prostitucion-la-paz-de-las-mujeres. Accessed on October 9, 2021.

Farley, Melissa. "Prostitución, tráfico y estrés postraumático." 2004. https://archivo.argentina.indymedia.org/uploads/2011/06/farley_cast.pdf. Accessed on October 9, 2021.

Gaceta de Madrid. Issue 181. June 1935. https://www.boe.es/datos/pdfs/BOE//1935/181/A02556-02558.pdf. Accessed on October 9, 2021.

Kraus, Ingeborg. "La prostitución es incompatible con la igualdad entre hombres y mujeres." 2016. Spanish translation by Maura Lopez. https://traductorasparaaboliciondelaprostitucion.weebly.com/blog/dra-ingeborg-kraus-la-prostitucion-es-incompatible-con-la-igualdad-entre-hombres-y-mujeres. Accessed on October 9, 2021.

MDM Navarra. "Entrevista sobre la trata de personas con la psicóloga jurídica y forense Laura Redondo." *Médicos del mundo*. Julio de 2019. http://www.medicosdelmundo.es/blogosfera/navarra/2019/07/30/1614/. Accessed on October 9, 2021.

Miguel Álvarez, Ana de. "La prostitución de mujeres, una escuela de desigualdad humana." *Revista Europea de Derechos Fundamentales*. Issue 19. 2012. https://mujeresenred.net/IMG/pdf/prostitucion_de_mujeres_escuela_desigualdad_humana.pdf. Accessed on October 9, 2021.

Miguel Álvarez, Ana de; Palomo Cermeño, Eva. "Los inicios de la lucha feminista contra la prostitución: políticas de redefinición y políticas activistas en el sufragismo inglés." *Cuadernos de Investigación Histórica*. Issue 35. 2011. https://publicaciones.unirioja.es/ojs/index.php/brocar/article/view/1609. Accessed on October 9, 2021.

Mujeres libres. "Liberatorios de prostitución." *FondationBesnard.org*. June 2016. http://www.fondation-besnard.org/spip.php?article2701. Accessed on October 9, 2021.

Pankhurst, Christabel. *The Great Scourge and How to End It*. 1913. https://iiif.wellcomecollection.org/pdf/b28093318. Accessed on October 9, 2021.

Resolución del Parlamento Europeo, de 26 de febrero de 2014, sobre explotación sexual y prostitución y su impacto en la igualdad de género. https://www.europarl.europa.eu/doceo/document/TA-7-2014-0162_ES.html?redirect. Accessed on October 9, 2021.

Rivas Arjona, Mercedes. "II República Española y Prostitución. El camino hacia la aprobación del decreto abolicionista en 1935." https://revistaseug.ugr.es/index.php/arenal/article/download/1570/1775. Accessed on October 9, 2021.

Tristan, Flora. "VIII. Mujeres públicas." *Paseos en Londres*. 1840. *https://www.marxists.org/espanol/tristan/1840/londres/viii.htm*. Accessed on October 9, 2021.

Tur, Francesc. "El debate sobre la prostitución durante la Segunda República." *Ser histórico. Portal de historia*. 2018 https://serhistorico.net/2018/10/25/el-debate-sobre-la-prostitucion-durante-la-segunda-republica/comment-page-1/. Accessed on October 9, 2021.

Wollstonecraft, Mary. "Vindicación de los derechos de la mujer." 1792. https://teoriapoliticaseminariohome.files.wordpress.com/2020/02/vindicacic3b3n_de_los_derechos_de_la_mujer.pdf. Accessed on October 9, 2021.

NOTES

1   The Declaration of Olympe de Gouges [in Spanish] can be reviewed at: http://clio.rediris.es/n31/derechosmujer.pdf.

2   The vindication of Mary Wollstonecraft at: https://teoriapoliticaseminariohome.files.wordpress.com/2020/02/vindicacic3b3n_de_los_derechos_de_la_mujer.pdf.

3   Complete text of chapter VIII of the work of Flora Tristan at: https://www.marxists.org/espanol/tristan/1840/londres/viii.htm.

4   Tristán, Flora op. cit. chapter VIII.

5   Tristán, Flora op. cit. chapter VIII.

6   Tristán, Flora op. cit. chapter VIII.

7   Miguel Álvarez, Ana de; Palomo Cermeño, Eva. "Los inicios de la lucha feminista contra la prostitución: políticas de redefinición y políticas activistas en el sufragismo inglés." *Cuadernos*

de Investigación Histórica. 35. 2011. https://publicaciones.unirioja.es/ojs/index.php/brocar/article/view/1609.

8   More about Butler's work at: https://revistaseug.ugr.es/index.php/arenal/article/download/1570/1775.

9   Pankhurst, Christabel. *The Great Scourge and How to End It*. 1913. https://iiif.wellcomecollection.org/pdf/b28093318.

10 Bacchiega, Julia: "Liberando esclavas" http://sedici.unlp.edu.ar/handle/10915/67733.

11 Convención Internacional para la Supresión de la Trata de Mujeres y Menores. https://www.senado.gob.mx/comisiones/desarrollo_social/docs/marco/Convencion_ITM.pdf.

12 Convenio para la represión de la trata de personas y de la explotación de la prostitución ajena https://www.ohchr.org/sp/professionalinterest/pages/trafficinpersons.aspx.

13 Castejon Bolea, Ramon. "Las enfermedades venéreas y la regulación de la sexualidad en la España contemporánea." *Asclepio*. Issue LVI-2. 2004. https://asclepio.revistas.csic.es/index.php/asclepio/article/view/45/44.

14 Castejon Bolea, Ramon. Op. Cit.

15 Tur, Francesc. "El debate sobre la prostitución durante la Segunda República." *Ser histórico. Portal de historia*. 2018 https://serhistorico.net/2018/10/25/el-debate-sobre-la-prostitucion-durante-la-segunda-republica/comment-page-1/

16 *Gaceta de Madrid*. Issue 181. June 1935. https://www.boe.es/datos/pdfs/BOE//1935/181/A02556-02558.pdf .

17 Bernal Triviño, Ana Isabel. "Cuando la República dijo sí a la abolición de la prostitución." *Publico.es*. November 11, 2018. https://www.publico.es/sociedad/abolicionismo-republica-dijo-abolicion-prostitucion.html.

18 All issues of "Mujeres Libres" (1936-1939) can be consulted at: https://cgt.org.es/revista-mujeres-libres/.

19 Mujeres libres. "Liberatorios de prostitución." *FondationBesnard.org*. June 2016. http://www.fondation-besnard.org/spip.php?article2701.

20 Sociologist Rosa Cobo Bedia explains this in her book *La Prostitución en el Corazón del Capitalismo* (2017) [Prostitution at the heart of capitalism].

21 MDM Navarra. "Entrevista sobre la trata de personas con la psicóloga jurídica y forense Laura Redondo." *Médicos del mundo*. July 2019. http://www.medicosdelmundo.es/blogosfera/navarra/2019/07/30/1614/.

22 Farley, Melissa. "Prostitución, tráfico y estrés postraumático." 2004. https://archivo.argentina.indymedia.org/uploads/2011/06/farley_cast.pdf.

23 Kraus, Ingeborg. "La prostitución es incompatible con la igualdad entre hombres y mujeres 2016. Spanish translation by Maura Lopez. https://traductorasparaaboliciondelaprostitucion.weebly.com/blog/dra-ingeborg-kraus-la-prostitucion-es-incompatible-con-la-igualdad-entre-hombres-y-mujeres.

24 Miguel Álvarez, Ana de. "La prostitución de mujeres, una escuela de desigualdad humana." *Revista Europea de Derechos Fundamentales*. Issue 19. 2012. https://mujeresenred.net/IMG/pdf/prostitucion_de_mujeres_escuela_desigualdad_humana.pdf.

25 The Regional Law 3/2018, dated April 19, for the Modification of the Regional Law 14/2015, dated April 10, to fight violence against women acknowledges that prostitution

and/or sexual exploitation are a for of violence against women and, therefore, prostituted women have a right to access resources in the same way that do other women victims of sexist violence. Full text at: http://www.lexnavarra.navarra.es/detalle.asp?r=50087.

26 Eckberg, Gunilla S. "El abordaje sueco de la prostitución: la paz de las mujeres." 2019. Translated into Spanish by Hinaetefaton Tebas. https://traductorasparaaboliciondelaprostitucion.weebly.com/blog/el-abordaje-sueco-de-la-prostitucion-la-paz-de-las-mujeres.

27 Eckberg, Gunilla S. Op. Cit.

28 Resolución del Parlamento Europeo, de 26 de febrero de 2014, sobre explotación sexual y prostitución y su impacto en la igualdad de género. https://www.europarl.europa.eu/doceo/document/TA-7-2014-0162_ES.html.

29 ¿Qué es el modelo nórdico? *Traductoras para la abolición de la prostitución.* https://traductorasparaaboliciondelaprostitucion.weebly.com/blog/que-es-el-modelo-nordico. And The Regional Law 3/2018, dated April 19, for the Modification of the Regional Law 14/2015, dated April 10, to fight violence against women. The French Law can be consulted at: http://www.cap-international.org/wp-content/uploads/2017/06/CAP-brochure-MAi2017esV3.pdf.

30 More information at: https://aboliciondelaprostitucion.wordpress.com/

31 "La PAP ha celebrado en Madrid un Encuentro para avanzar en la organización abolicionista." *AmecoPress. Información para la ligualdad.* December 2019. https://amecopress.net/El-pasado-fin-de-semana-tuvo-lugar-en-Madrid.

32 Presentación pública de la ley abolicionista. *Por la abolición de la prostitución.* March 2020. https://aboliciondelaprostitucion.wordpress.com/2020/03/06/presentacion-publica-de-la-ley-abolicionista/

33 All the information about the LOASP can be accessed at www.leyabolicionista.es.

34 The Regional Law 3/2018, dated April 19, for the Modification of the Regional Law 14/2015, dated April 10, to fight violence against women.

35 "El Gobierno de Navarra se suma al Día Internacional contra la Explotación Sexual y la Trata de Personas y expresa su firme compromiso en la erradicación de esta violencia contra las mujeres". *Navarra.es.* September 2020. https://www.navarra.es/es/noticias/2020/09/23/el-gobierno-de-navarra-se-suma-al-dia-internacional-contra-la-explotacion-sexual-y-la-trata-de-personas-y-expresa-su-firme-compromiso-en-la-erradicacion-de-esta-violencia-contra-las-mujeres.

Biographies

(in alphabetical order)

Sarah Jane Blithe

Sarah Jane Blithe (PhD, University of Colorado, Boulder) is associate professor of communication studies at the University of Nevada, Reno. Her expertise is in organizational communication, with specific attention to intersectional gender, work-life balance, policy inequalities, and management learning. Blithe is the author of *Gender Equality and Work-Life Balance: Glass Handcuffs and Working Men in the U.S.* and *Sex and Stigma: Stories of Everyday Life in Nevada's Legal Brothels*, with Anna Wiederhold Wolfe and Breanna Mohr, both of which won multiple national book awards. She is also the co-editor of *Badass Feminist Politics: Exploring Radical Edges of Feminist Theory, Communication, and Activism*, published in 2021. Blithe is the recipient of multiple research and teaching awards, including the 2019 Thornton Peace Prize from the Nevada System of Higher Education, for her social justice advocacy.

Sydney Graham

Sydney Graham is a doctoral student at the University of Missouri in Columbia. Her work examines identification and stigmatization of women in organizational contexts, specifically the identity narratives of sex workers in Nevada's legal brothels. Before beginning the doctoral program at Mizzou, Graham served as the social media specialist at a private museum in Washington, DC.

Xabier Irujo

Born in exile in Caracas, Venezuela, in 1967, Xabier Irujo is the director of the Center for Basque Studies at the University of Nevada, Reno, where he is professor of genocide studies. He was the first guest research scholar of the Manuel Irujo Chair at the University of Liverpool and has taught seminars on genocide and cultural genocide at Boise State University and at the University of California, Santa Barbara. He holds three master's degrees in linguistics, history, and philosophy and has two PhDs in history and philosophy. Irujo has lectured in almost one hundred American and European universities and academic or cultural institutions (typically governments, parliaments, museums, and libraries.) He has published on issues related to Basque history and politics, including genocide studies with a focus on physical and cultural extermination.

He has mentored numerous graduate students and he is the member of the editorial board of four academic presses in Europe and the Americas. Irujo has authored more than fifteen books and a number of articles in journals, and he has received awards and honors at the national and international level. His recent books include *Gernika: Genealogy of a Lie* (Sussex Academic Press, 2018), *Gernika 1937: The Market Day Massacre* (University of Nevada Press, 2015) and *Charlemagne's Defeat in the Pyrenees: The Battle of Rencesvals* (Amsterdam University Press, Amsterdam, 2021).

Omita Joshi

Omita Joshi is a program officer at the Community Action Center (CAC)-Nepal, a non-governmental organization based in Kathmandu, Nepal, that provides health and social services to marginalized women in the community. Ms. Joshi has extensive knowledge and more than 20 years of experience in planning and implementing development programs for women and children at the grassroots, community, and national levels. She has also facilitated community-based research for educational institutions and international organizations such as the Nepal Medical College, USAID, and FHI360. Ms. Joshi holds a master's degree in health care management from Pokhara University, Nepal.

Rebecca J. Meisenbach

Rebecca J. Meisenbach (PhD, Purdue University, 2004) is an associate professor at the University of Missouri in Columbia. Her research addresses issues of ethics and marginalized or stigmatized identity in relation to our organizational lives. Current projects focus on theorizing stigma as a power-laden communicative process. Her work has been published in outlets such as *Communication Monographs*, rhe *International Journal of Strategic Communication*, the *Journal of Applied Communication Research, Management Communication Quarterly*, and *Sex Roles*. Meisenbach is currently the editor-in-chief for *Management Communication Quarterly* and teaches undergraduate courses such as organizational advocacy, communication theory, and organizational communication, as well as graduate courses in communication theory, organizational communication, and stigma.

Silvia Pérez Freire

Silvia Pérez Freire holds a doctorate in sociology. An associate lecturer at the University of Vigo since 2007, she has been a social researcher specializing in gender violence for the last seventeen years. Pérez has coordinated programs for populations of women in prostitution in the feminist Association (Asociación feminista Alecrín) in Galicia from 2003 to 2008, and she is the cofounder of the Galician Network against sexual trafficking since 2008. She works as an independent sociologist for several Spanish universities, nongovernmental organizations, research institutions, and for the public administration. Pérez is a member of the Red Iberoamericana de Imaginary y Representations (RIIR) and is the chief executive officer of the Spanish company Rizoma Social S.L. (www.rizomasocial.gal). She has published eleven books and more than twenty academic papers. She has participated in more than twenty social research projects in her field, primarily about prostitution and sexuality, and equality and gender violence.

Yerina S. Ranjit

Yerina S. Ranjit is an assistant professor of health communication in the Department of Communication at the University of Missouri. Ranjit's (PhD, University of Connecticut, 2016) research program focuses on behavior change communication in the context of health. As a communication scholar, she has examined the role of mediated communication in improving health in the underserved populations, such as among people with HIV who use drugs, female sex workers in developing countries, women in prison, and young men who have sex with men (YMSM). As a trainee of public health at Yale School of Medicine, her line of inquiry was to understand the prevalence and enabling and disabling factors of infectious diseases, mainly HIV, both in the national and international contexts. Ranjit's work has been published in the *Journal of Health Communication*, *AIDS and Behavior*, the *Journal of Computer Mediated Communication*, and *Stigma and Health*.

Yolanda Rodríguez Villegas

Delegate of the Women's Platform for the Abolition of Prostitution of Navarra (PNAP), historian, librarian, and activist, Yolanda Rodríguez Villegas is the founder of the Navarra Women's Platform for the Abolition of Prostitution. For ten years she was a volunteer and partner of World Doctors of Navarre, and from 2014 to 2019 she became the president of this nongovernmental organization. She has a master's in gender studies from the Public University of Navarra, and offers training lectures on prostitution, trafficking, and sexual exploitation. She has written numerous articles on the subject in specialized journals and mainstream media. As a member of the PNAP, she has participated as an expert advisor for the drafting of the Organic Law to Abolish the Prostitution System presented in November 2020.

Sara Vicente Collado

Sara Vicente Collado is a lawyer specializing in family law, violence against women, and criminal law. Since 1996 she has belonged to the Commission for the Investigation of Mistreatment of Women and has promoted various organizations and programs dedicated to the examination of prostitution in the Basque Country and in Spain. She has trained professionals on violence against women. She opened a legal office in Madrid in 2001 and in Pamplona in 2013, and she has advised women intervening in legal proceedings in defense of their rights to a life free of violence. She is the author of numerous articles, communications, and book chapters related to violence against women, violence in intimate relationships, sexual violence, prostitution, and trafficking for sexual exploitation.

Amelia Walker

Amelia Walker is a graduate student earning her master's degree from the Communication Studies Department at the University of Nevada, Reno. She is a sex worker, human rights activist, and critical intercultural communication scholar. Her research interests are rooted in feminist and queer theories. She is specifically focused on the ways in which deviant bodies disrupt social norms. Walker is a sex work advocate committed to challenging stigma against minority groups and exposing the power dynamics that harm vulnerable communities.

Index

abolitionism, 108–25
  agency, autonomy, and, 40
  basic tenets of, 116–17
  in Basque Country, x–xi, 80–81, 82, 83, 121–25
  client and demand opposition with, 109–11, 115, 117–24
  European model of, xi, xii, 83, 117–18
  feminist perspective and advocacy on, ix, 40, 80, 108–14, 117, 119, 121–22
  legal status and, ix, 109, 111–12, 117–18
  in Navarra/Nafarroa, 121–25
  Nordic model of, xii, 117–18
  Organic Law for, xii, 80–81, 119–21, 122, 124
  organizational advocacy for, 26–28, 31
  pimping opposition with, 109–11, 116, 117, 119–21, 123
  prohibition compared, ix, 114–15
  regulationism compared, 115–16
  social support goals with, 117–18, 119–20, 124–25
advertising, of sex work, 3, 42–43, 70, 80–82, 121, 123
advocacy
  for abolitionism, ix–xii, 26–28, 31, 40, 80–83, 108–25
  ideological perspectives of, viii–x
  on legal status, viii–ix, 12, 20, 22, 40, 55 (see also abolitionism; prohibitionism; regulationism)
  organizational support and (see organizational support)
  for prohibitionism, ix, 27–28, 82–83, 114–15
  for sex workers' health, 29–30, 31
  for sex workers' rights, 28–29, 31, 34, 41, 52
  for social support, 24–26, 31–34, 99–100, 117–18, 119–20, 124–25
agency and autonomy, 40–62
  benefits to personal, 54–55
  censorship affecting, 43, 49, 55–56
  exploitation and, 41, 49–50, 52–55, 58
  ideological advocacy on, viii–ix
  income (in)stability and, 42, 43, 51, 54–56
  job autonomy, 46, 54–55
  legal status and, 12, 40, 41–43, 47–50, 55, 57–58
  legislation and policies affecting, 40–41, 42–43, 47–50, 52–53, 55–58
  marginalization affecting, 40–41, 52–53, 55–56
  morality views and, 42, 53–54, 55–56
  obstacles to personal, 55–56
  organizational stances on, 28–29, 31–34, 41
  pleasure and, 46–47, 54–55
  research and scholarship on, xi, 40–62
    analysis of findings, 56–57
    discussion topics, 46–56
    future, 57–58
    limitations, 57
    methodology, 44–45
    research questions, 44
    results, 45–46, 58–62
  sex work as legitimate work and, 41, 52, 54–55
  sex work vs. sex trafficking distinction and, 50–51, 55–56
  stigma and, 40–41, 48–49, 52–56
anti-prostitution advocacy, ix–x. *See also* abolitionism; prohibitionism
anti-prostitution legislation, 49–50
anti-trafficking legislation
  agency and autonomy effects of, 41, 42–43, 47–50, 52–53, 55, 57–58
  Basque Country prostitution and, 74–80
Asia Pacific Network of Sex Workers (APNSW), 29
Awaken, 27

Backpage, 43
Basque Country prostitution, 67–83
  abolition of, x–xi, 80–81, 82, 83, 121–25
  characteristics of, 67–68
  client/customer statistics for, x, 68, 70, 81
  context for, x–xii, 67
  COVID-19 pandemic and, 70, 73

demographics of, 67–74, 81, 85n3
economics of, 68, 69, 71–72, 73, 80, 82
health issues and, 72–74, 76
immigration and, 67, 69, 71, 72–74, 76, 81–82
models of regulation for, 82–83
placement system in, 69
recruitment of sex workers for, 74, 81
regulation and legal status of, 74–83
sex trafficking and, x, 67, 69–70, 72–83
violence and, 72–73, 75–80, 82
Beijing Declaration and Platform for Action (1995), 75
blackmail, 7–8
Blithe, Sarah Jane, vii, xi, 22

CAC (Communication Action Center)-Nepal, 5, 15
censorship, 43, 49, 55–56
Chicago Alliance Against Sexual Exploitation, 27–28
clients
    abolitionist stance on, 109–11, 115, 117–24
    Basque Country/Spanish statistics on, x, 68, 70, 81, 101
    blackmail by/of, 7–8
    death threats from, 8–9
    demand from, 80, 93, 100–101, 103, 109–10, 115, 117–24
    as first-order observers, 91, 99–100
    invisibility of, 101–4
    screening of, 42, 43
    Swedish legal model penalizing, xii, 3, 82, 83, 117–18
    transference of responsibility from, xii, 91, 101–4, 105
    violence and safety issues with (see safety; violence)
Communication Action Center (CAC)-Nepal, 5, 15
consent, viii–ix, 50, 75–76, 79–80, 95–96, 109–10, 116
Convention against Transnational Organized Crime (2000), 75
Convention for the Suppression of the Traffic in Persons and the Exploitation of the Prostitution of Others (1949), 74, 76, 111, 117
Convention on Preventing and Combating Violence Against Women and Domestic Violence (Istanbul Convention, 2011), 76–77

Convention on the Elimination of All Forms of Discrimination against Women (1979), 75
COYOTE (Call Off Your Old Tired Ethics), 29
Craigslist, 43
Criminal Act of 2017 (Nepal), 3
criminalization
    abolitionism and, xii, 83, 114–15, 117, 120
    agency and autonomy affected by, xi, 41–42, 47–50, 55–58
    legal status and, xi, 1–3, 11–12, 18–20 (see also legal status of sex work)
    prohibitionism and, ix, 27–28, 82–83, 114–15
    social imaginaries and transference of responsibility related to, xii, 91, 98, 101–4, 105
critical thematic analysis (CTA), xi, 44–45, 56–58

death threats, 8–9
decriminalization and legalization
    abolitionism and, 115–16, 117–18
    advocacy for, ix, 3, 12, 22, 28–29, 40, 42, 47–50, 54–55, 115–16, 118
    agency and autonomy arguments for, ix, 28, 40–42, 47–50, 54–55
    legal status and, xi, 2, 3–4, 6, 12, 18, 20 (see also legal status of sex work)
    organizational support for, 22, 28–29
    social imaginaries and, 102
Desiree Alliance, 29
dirty work, viii, 1–2, 18, 23. See also emotional taint; moral taint; physical taint; social taint
dissociation, 102, 103, 105, 116
double standards, 92, 109
Durbar Mahila Samanwaya Committee, 29

Eaves' Poppy Project, 27
Emakunde, 68, 69, 78, 81
emotional taint, viii, 23
exploitation
    abolitionism to avoid (see abolitionism)
    agency, autonomy, and, 41, 49–50, 52–55, 58
    in Basque Country prostitution, 68, 74, 76–79
    defined, 49
    organizational stances on, 27–28, 31
    social imaginaries of prostitution and, 91, 94–100, 103–6

Facebook, 43
feminist theory/perspective
    on abolitionism, ix, 40, 80, 108–14, 117, 119, 121–22

on agency and autonomy of sex workers, 40–45, 57, 58
on social imaginaries of prostitution, 92, 93
feminization of poverty, x, 80, 109, 115, 122
FOSTA (Fight Online Sex Trafficking Act), 42–43, 47–50, 52–53, 55
France, legal status of sex work in, 82, 83
Free Women (Mujeres Libres), 112–14

Global Health Justice Partnership (GHJP), 30
Global Network of Sex Work Projects (NSWP), 28
Google, 43
Graham, Sydney, xi, 1

health
 abolitionist stance on prostitute treatment for, 109–10, 111–12
 Basque Country prostitution and, 72–74, 76
 dissociation effects on, 102, 103, 105, 116
 health insurance, 4
 legal status of sex work and, 1, 4, 5, 7, 13–18, 19
 organizational advocacy for, 29–30, 31
 PTSD effects on, 115–16
 social support lack affecting, 25
 STIs and, 4, 5, 13–17, 30, 72, 109–10, 111–12 (*see also* HIV)
HIV, 4, 5, 7, 13–15, 17, 30, 101
human trafficking. *See* sex trafficking
Human Trafficking and Transportation Act of 2007 (Nepal), 3

identity
 disclosure of, as sex worker, 6–11, 18–19, 48
 marginalization based on, 40–41, 52–53, 55–56
 occupational, 24
income
 autonomy and (in)stability of, 42, 43, 51, 54–56
 in Basque Country prostitution, 69, 71
independent contractor status, x, 4, 17, 34
Instagram, 43
Instituto Vasco de la Mujer, 78
International Abolitionist Federation, 110
International Convention against Trafficking in Human Beings (2005), 76–77
International Convention for the Suppression of Traffic in Women and Children, 111
International Day Against the Sexual Exploitation of Women and Children, 80, 110
International Day Against Trafficking in Persons, 69, 80

Internet platforms. *See* online platforms
Irujo, Xabier, vii, xi–xii, 67
Istanbul Convention (2011), 76–77

job autonomy, 46, 54–55
johns. *See* clients

labor unions, 34
law enforcement agencies
 Basque Country prostitution and access to, 71, 78, 82
 legal status of sex work and interactions with, ix, 11–12, 16, 17
 social imaginaries of prostitution and, 96–100, 104, 105
legal status of sex work, 1–20. *See also* criminalization; decriminalization and legalization
 abolitionist stance on, ix, 109, 111–12, 117–18 (*see also* abolitionism)
 advocacy and organizational support on, viii–ix, 12, 20, 22, 40, 55
 agency, autonomy, and, 12, 40, 41–43, 47–50, 55, 57–58
 in Basque Country, 75, 76, 82, 83
 disclosure of sex worker identity and, 6–11, 18–19
 health and, 1, 4, 5, 7, 13–18, 19
 law enforcement interactions and, ix, 11–12, 16, 17
 in Nepal, xi, 2–3, 4–20
 in Nevada brothels, x, xi, 3–20
 organizational stances on, 27, 28, 34
 prohibitionist stance on, ix, 27–28, 82–83, 114–15
 research and study of, 4–20
  analysis techniques, 6
  data procedures, 5–6
  on identity, health, and law enforcement, 6–18
  methodology, 4–5
  participants, 5
  summary of findings, 18–20
 social imaginaries of prostitution and, xii, 91, 95–96, 102
 stigma, taints, and, ix, xi, 1–2, 4–5, 8, 18–20, 55
LOASP (Organic Law for the Abolition of the Prostitution System), xii, 80–81, 119–21, 122, 124
lockdown policies, x, 4, 17

marginalization, 40–41, 52–53, 55–56
Marxist feminists, stance of, 41

Meisenbach, Rebecca J., xi, 1
morality
    abolitionist stance on, ix, 110
    agency, autonomy, and, 42, 53–54, 55–56
    defined, 53
moral taint, viii, 2, 4, 18, 19–20, 23
Mujeres Libres (Free Women), 112–14

naming, 92, 94–95
National Association of Women for the Revoking
        of the Law of Contagious Diseases, 110
Nepal
    criminalization of prostitution in, 2–3, 11–12
    disclosure of sex worker identity in, 6–9, 19
    health of sex workers in, 5, 7, 13–16, 19
    law enforcement interactions in, 11–12, 16
    research on sex work in, xi, 4–20
Nevada
    disclosure of sex worker identity in, 9–11, 18–19
    health of sex workers in, 4, 16–18, 19
    law enforcement interactions in, 12, 17
    legalized prostitution in brothels in, x, 3–4, 12
    organizational support in, 27, 29
    research on sex work in, x, xi, 4–20
Norway, legal status of sex work in, 118
NSWP (Global Network of Sex Work Projects),
        28

occupational identity, 24
Onesta Foundation, 29
online platforms
    advertising via, 42, 43, 70, 82
    anti-trafficking legislation addressing, 42–43,
        47–48
    censorship of, 43, 49, 55–56
    pornography on, 81
    recruitment of sex workers via, 74
    research via, xi, 43–62
    sex work via, 42–43, 50–51, 55–56, 67, 71, 103
OnlyFans, 74
Organic Law for the Abolition of the Prostitution
        System (LOASP), xii, 80–81, 119–21, 122, 124
organizational support, 22–34. See also advocacy
    overview, xi, 22–23
    for abolitionism, 26–28, 31
    fractured theories of, 26–31
    "framing battle" in, 22
    practical contributions of research on, 33–34
    for prohibitionism, 27–28
    for sex workers' health, 29–30, 31

sex workers' involvement in, 34, 58
for sex workers' rights, 28–29, 31, 34, 41
social imaginaries of prostitution influencing,
        99–100, 105
as social support, 24–26, 31–34, 99–100, 124
stigma and, 22, 23–24, 29–31, 33–34
summary of findings on, 31–34
theoretical contributions of research on, 32–33
violence and safety issues and, 22, 24, 27–28, 30, 124

Palacios Law of 1913 (Argentina), 110
PAP (State Platform of Women for the Abolition
        of Prostitution), 80, 119, 122
patriarchal context
    for abolitionism, x, 120–22
    agency and autonomy despite, 41, 54
    for Basque Country prostitution, xii
    demand for prostitution reflecting, 115
    for social imaginaries of prostitution, xii, 91, 93,
        94–96, 105
PayPal, 42
people of color, sex workers as, vii, 24, 57–58
Pérez Freire, Silvia, xii, 91
person-centered messages, 25–26, 31–34
physical taint, viii, 2, 18, 23
pimps
    abolitionist stance on, 109–11, 116, 117, 119–21, 123
    agency and autonomy from, 50 (see also agency
        and autonomy)
    in Basque Country prostitution, 68–69, 71, 73,
        123
    as first-order observers, 91, 99–100
    legal status of sex work and, 3, 12, 95, 117
    prohibition against, 27
    social imaginaries of prostitution and, 91, 95,
        99–100
Platform for the Abolition of Prostitution,
        Navarra Women's (PNAP), 80, 121
Platform of Women for the Abolition of
        Prostitution, State (PAP), 80, 119, 122
pleasure, 46–47, 54–55
police. See law enforcement agencies
post-traumatic stress disorder (PTSD), 115–16
privacy issues, 9
prohibitionism, ix, 27–28, 82–83, 114–15
prostitution. See also sex work; sex workers
    overview of research on, vii–xiii
    anti-prostitution advocacy, ix–x (see also
        abolitionism; prohibitionism)
    anti-prostitution legislation, 49–50

in Basque Country, x–xii, 67–83, 85n3, 121–25
defined, 2, 93
economics of, vii
legal status of (*see* legal status of sex work)
social imaginaries of, xii, 91–106
terminology for, vii–viii
Prostitution Liberatoriums, 113–14
Prostitution Research and Education, 27
Protocol for Coordination and Action with Women and Girl Victims of Trafficking for the Purpose of Sexual Exploitation (2016), 79
PTSD (post-traumatic stress disorder), 115–16
Public Entertainment and Recreational Activities Bill of 2018 (Basque), 78
Public Offense and Penalties Act (Nepal), 3

radical feminists, stance of, ix, 41. *See also* feminist theory/perspective
radical libertarian advocacy, viii–ix
Ranjit, Yerina S., xi, 1
rape and sexual assault, 16, 19, 80, 82
Red de Mujeres Trabajadoras Sexuales de Latinoamérica y el Caribe (RedTraSex), 29
Reddit, xi, 43–44
Red Umbrella Fund, 28
regulationism, xi, 115–16
religious affiliations, ix, 10
Rodríguez Villegas, Yolanda, vii, xii, 108
Roux, Liara, 43
Roux's Ask Me Anything, 43–62
Russia, prohibitionism in, 82–83

safety
anti-trafficking legislation affecting, 42–43, 52–53
client screening for, 42, 43
death threats and, 8–9
disclosure of identity as sex worker and, 8–11, 18–19
online sex work improving, 42
organizational support to improve, 24, 27–28, 124
stigma affecting, 48–49
violence threatening (*see* violence)
St. James Infirmary, 30
Scarlet Alliance, 29
SESTA (Stop Enabling Sex Traffickers Act), 42–43, 47–50, 52–53, 55
"sex positive" advocacy, viii–ix
sex trafficking

abolitionism to avoid, ix, 110–11, 117–18, 124 (*see also* abolitionism)
anti-trafficking legislation, 41, 42–43, 47–50, 52–53, 55, 57–58, 74–80
Basque Country prostitution and, x, 67, 69–70, 72–83
defined, 75–76, 95–96
legitimacy of sex work reducing, 52
organizational stances on sex work as, 27, 28, 31–32
sex work conflated with, ix–x, 3, 4, 20, 27, 42, 49–50, 116–17
sex work distinction from, 50–51, 55–56
social imaginaries of prostitution and, 91, 94–100, 106
Spanish laws and policies on, 75–76, 77, 95, 98
statistics on, ix–x
sexual exploitation. *See* exploitation
sexually transmitted infections (STIs), 4, 5, 13–17, 30, 72, 109–10, 111–12. *See also* HIV
sexual tourism, 118, 123
sex work. *See also* prostitution; sex workers
overview of research on, vii–xiii
abolition of (*see* abolitionism)
advertising of, 3, 42–43, 70, 80–82, 121, 123
defined, vii–viii, 1, 40
as dirty work, viii, 1–2, 18, 23
legal status (*see* legal status of sex work)
as legitimate work, viii, 28, 31, 33, 41, 52, 54–55
online, 42–43, 50–51, 55–56, 67, 71, 103
prohibition of, ix, 27–28, 82–83, 114–15
sex trafficking and (*see* sex trafficking)
terminology for, vii–viii
sex workers. *See also* prostitution; sex work
advocacy by/for (*see* advocacy)
agency and autonomy of (*see* agency and autonomy)
blackmail of, 7–8
clients of (*see* clients)
of color, vii, 24, 57–58
disclosure of identity as, 6–11, 18–19, 48
exploitation of (*see* exploitation)
factors influencing, vii
health of (*see* health)
as independent contractors, x, 4, 17, 34
law enforcement interactions with (*see* law enforcement agencies)
organizational support for (*see* organizational support)
rights of, advocacy for, 28–29, 31, 34, 41, 52

safety of (*see* safety)
stigma experienced by (*see* stigma)
terminology for, xi
transgender (*see* transgender sex workers)
violence toward (*see* violence)
Sex Workers Education and Advocacy Taskforce (SWEAT), 29
social imaginaries of prostitution, 91–106
   overview, xii, 91–94
   client invisibility and, 101–4
   defined, 92
   devaluation of life in, 104–6
   double standards and, 92
   first-order observers in, xii, 91, 93, 96–100, 105
   gender inequities and, 92–93, 105
   law enforcement interactions and, 96–100, 104, 105
   legal status and, xii, 91, 95–96, 102
   naming in, importance of, 92, 94–95
   objectification in, 104–6
   organizational support influenced by, 99–100, 105
   patriarchal context for, xii, 91, 93, 94–96, 105
   research participants on, 93–94
   social magma of prostitution and, 106
   transference of responsibility and victimization in, xii, 91, 101–4, 105
social media platforms. *See* online platforms
social support
   abolitionist stance on, 117–18, 119–20, 124–25
   organizational support as, 24–26, 31–34, 99–100, 124
   social imaginaries of prostitution influencing, 99–100
social taint, viii, 2, 4, 18, 23
stigma
   agency, autonomy, and, 40–41, 48–49, 52–56
   defined, 1, 48
   dirty work and, viii, 1–2, 18, 23 (*see also* emotional taint; moral taint; physical taint; social taint)
   experiences with, varying, viii, x
   of homosexuality, 8
   legal status of sex work and, ix, xi, 1–2, 4–5, 8, 18–20, 55
   legitimacy of sex work reducing, viii, 52, 54
   marginalization with, 40–41, 52, 55–56
   morality views driving, 53–54, 56 (*see also* moral taint)

organizational support and, 22, 23–24, 29–31, 33–34
   symbolic, viii, 23
   whore, viii, 23, 40
STIs (sexually transmitted infections), 4, 5, 13–17, 30, 72, 109–10, 111–12. *See also* HIV
Stop Enabling Sex Traffickers Act (SESTA), 42–43, 47–50, 52–53, 5
SWEAT (Sex Workers Education and Advocacy Taskforce), 29
Sweden, legal status of sex work in, xii, 3, 82, 83, 117–18
symbolic stigma, viii, 23

TikTok, 74
trafficking. *See* sex trafficking
transgender sex workers
   in Basque Country prostitution, 68
   disclosure of identity as, 7, 8
   health experiences of, 7, 15–16, 30
   law enforcement interactions with, 11
   legal status of sex work and, 3, 7, 8, 11, 15–16
   stigma of, 8
   violence toward, vii, 24
Twitter, 43

venereal infections. *See* sexually transmitted infections
VerifyHim, 43
Vik, Tennley A., xi, 22
violence
   abolitionist stance on, 117, 120–23
   anti-trafficking legislation goals of reducing, 75–80
   Basque Country prostitution and, 72–73, 75–80, 82
   death threats, 8–9
   experiences with, varying, vii, x
   legal status of sex work and, ix, xii, 8–9, 16, 19
   organizational support against, 22, 24, 27–28, 30
   outing as, 48
   rape and sexual assault as, 16, 19, 80, 82
   safety from (*see* safety)
   sources of, 24

Walker, Amelia, xi, 40
whore stigma, viii, 23, 40
World Health Organization (WHO), 30

www.ingramcontent.com/pod-product-compliance
Lightning Source LLC
Chambersburg PA
CBHW070807240726
48654CB00007B/245